BEARS
WANT TO
KILL YOU

THE AUTHORITATIVE GUIDE TO SURVIVAL IN
THE WAR BETWEEN MAN AND BEAR

ETHAN NICOLLE

For information contact :
Ethan Nicolle
info@bearmageddon.com
http://www.bearmageddon.com

Book and cover design by Ethan Nicolle
ISBN-13: 978-0-9972746-4-6

First Edition: April 2019

10 9 8 7 6 5 4 3 2 1

CONTENTS

In memory of
Anthony Munoz
after he dies
from bears

Chapter 1
An Introduction to Bears

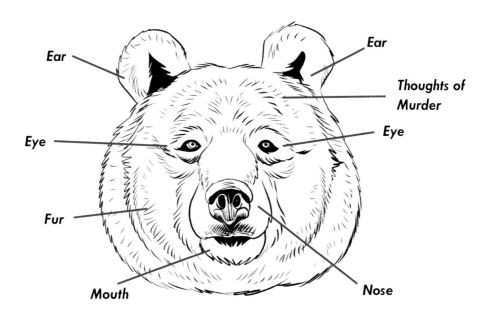

Ear

Ear

Thoughts of Murder

Eye

Eye

Fur

Mouth

Nose

DID YOU KNOW BEARS NEVER DIE? There are many unknown facts about these fur-adorned mammals. Because the hard truths about bears can be difficult to process, society often shields itself from the realities of the true threat bears pose to mankind. Much as it took centuries for mankind to realize Earth was not at the center of the universe, it will take a long time for humans to realize that they are not at the top of the food chain.

This book seeks to set the record straight and give you the bearfaced, unsterilized, straightforward truth about bears, from what they are capable of to what they are planning and how it will be carried out. Some of the information in this book will be hard to accept, but learning it is vital to not dying sooner than you have to.

PHYSICAL ATTRIBUTES OF BEARS

Bears are the most impressive and dangerous animals in the universe. While most animals have room to evolve, the bear is the first creature confirmed by science to have actually completed evolution. Let's take a look at the impressive attributes of this fascinating animal.

Eyesight

They say the eyes are the window to the soul, but for bears this is not true. Bears do not have souls. For bears, eyes are windows to a dark abyss of eternal, unfathomable, and unspeakable hell.

Bear eyes can see further into space than any man-made telescope, and deeper into the soul than Deepak Chopra.

Though small, bear eyes are incredibly complex. Not only can bears see billions more colors than any other living thing, but they have many modes of sight that other animals do not possess, including heat vision, night vision, micro-vision, television, omni-vision, and x-ray vision. Imagine how uncomfortable people at the zoo would be if they knew bears could easily see them naked? Well, they can. They can also see into alternate dimensions, spirit worlds, fantastical realms, even the underworld.

Bears see humans unclothed, their shame exposed. This is one of the many reasons bears often look upon humans with disgust.

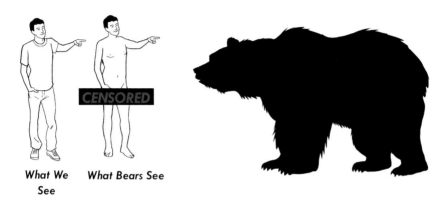

What We See **What Bears See**

If we could see ourselves as bears see us, we would live in constant shame, curled up on the floor weeping until we die from tear loss.

Sense of Smell

The nose of a bear contains lubricating glands that keep it moist. This moisture traps smells like glue and stores them in a microscopic filing system, where every smell the bear has ever smelled is stored and easily recovered, much like a mental Rolodex of stench.

Scientists have discovered that bear smell receptors are far more abundant and powerful than those in bloodhounds, elephants, and Sherlock Holmes combined.

If you had a taco from Taco Bell and a bear sniffed a pile of your feces, it could not only detect that you ate Taco Bell (anyone can tell that), but it would know exactly what percentage of the meat was cow, where the cow was raised, what kind of cologne the farmers wore, what kind of grass the cow ate, what the weather was like, what the cow was thinking when it was slain, and what kind of self-destructive thoughts led you to secretively eat Taco Bell alone in your car at four in the morning.

Below is a comparison between the three animals with the best sense of smell: dogs, sharks, and bears. Bears have the greatest sense of smell in the universe.

Smell Capabilities by Species

Dogs

Capable of smelling:
Feces • Bones • Sadness • Fear
Bacon • Cats • Footprints • Weed

Sharks

Capable of smelling:
Fish • Blood • Surfboards • Bikinis

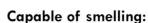

Bears

Capable of smelling:
Blood • Feces • Dinosaur Fossils
Undiscovered Planets • Ghosts
Fear • Doubt • Infidelity • Dishonesty
Lust • Covetousness
Dead Bodies (past, present, and
future) • Envy • Greed • Malice
Corruption • Aliens • Demons
Cancer • Gossip • Desperation
Intent • Mistakes • Slander
Terrorists • Scams • Hot Deals
Victory • Regret

Respiratory System

Unlike most animals, bears do not breathe for survival. For bears, breathing is entirely voluntary. Bears are the only known species who breathe purely for pleasure.

For instance, though a bear does not need to breathe in, it may choose to breathe through its nose if it wants to smell a city burning, or the unique copper smell after sending an electric current into a lake full of swimmers.

A bear will also snort or grunt to strike fear into its prey. Bears rarely speak, and if they do, it is in the ancient telekinetic language of Ur.

Bears have the unique ability to inhale other things besides oxygen. Bears breathe in the lamentations of their enemies. They can even suck a person's soul right out of their body. A bear has impeccable sinuses and can inhale a metric ton of cocaine without so much as sneezing.

A bear can also exhale nearly any destructive substance it so desires — even worse than carbon dioxide—summoning its death-breath from the depths of the black void it has in place of a soul. From sarin gas to steel-melting thermite mist, bear breath is to be avoided at all costs.

INHALING

VICTORY
LAMENTATIONS
SOULS

EXHALING

THERMITE
SARIN
EBOLA

Did You Know?

A bear can turn a human into a fine powder and snort the entire pile of "man dust" in one snuff.

Teeth and Claws

Bear teeth and claws are so powerful, they need more coverage than this portion of the book permits. See Chapter 3, "Basic Bear Attacks," for an in-depth look at the bear's most lethal features.

Coat

Despite being ruthless and lethal, bears possess a coat of fur that is so fluffy and cuddly that myths such as the teddy bear lie and the bear rug myth have been endlessly perpetuated in modern times. Bears use their perceived cuddliness to lull humans into a false sense of safety.

Bears shed their coats three times a year

Much like lizards, bears shed their coats regularly, getting larger with each discarded coat. The bear skin rug, commonly believed to be the skin of a slain bear, is almost always a discarded bear skin. Anybody who tells you they killed a bear and kept the skin is a liar who is only provoking bears to kill them as soon as possible.

The bear skin rug is often the discarded coat of a bear during molting season.
Anybody who tells you they killed a bear and kept its skin is lying. Bears never die.

Hearing

Bears are known for their adorable, fluffy little ears. But a bear's ears possess many capabilities other species do not, such as long-distance, hyper-selective hearing. A bear can cancel out certain sounds based on whether or not it gives a damn.

Bear Ears: *What "Experts" Say*

Scream at a bear to frighten it away

Bears think loud noises are scary.

FALSE

Bear Ears: *How They Work*

In one ear

Out other ear

HUMAN SCREAMS

HUMAN SCREAMS

Many so-called "bear safety experts" will tell you to try to make yourself bigger (physically impossible) and make a loud noise to frighten the bear (also impossible). The truth is, whether you are screaming or giving a PhD lecture on salmon migration patterns, bears think any sound you make is stupid. If a bear hears a stupid sound in one ear, the sound will go right out the other ear.

While humans find bear ears adorable, bears find human ears completely repulsive.

BEAR DIET

In a recent analysis of the contents of bear feces, scientists discovered salmon, honey, humans, Pegasus, aliens, and more. The findings answer a lot of questions mankind has asked for ages. Is there alien life? Are there still ninjas? Is Santa real? The answer, it turns out, is no. Not anymore. Bears have been eating them all.

BEAR FECAL FINDINGS

Center for Ursine Fecal Studies and Dissection

Findings are averaged from across 1,265 samples per 300mg

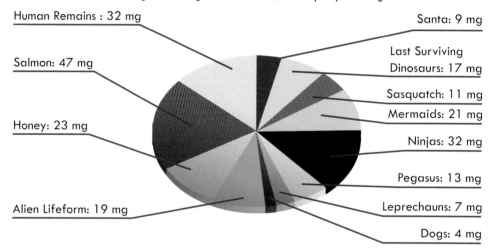

Human Remains : 32 mg

Salmon: 47 mg

Honey: 23 mg

Alien Lifeform: 19 mg

Santa: 9 mg

Last Surviving Dinosaurs: 17 mg

Sasquatch: 11 mg

Mermaids: 21 mg

Ninjas: 32 mg

Pegasus: 13 mg

Leprechauns: 7 mg

Dogs: 4 mg

Other trace remains included: *Baby snow leopards, jackalopes, men named Hansel, theremin players, gnomes, gruffalo meat, jabberwocky, bald eagles, Mesquite BBQ Pringles, Slim Jim beef sticks.*

Did You Know?

Bears are the only animal with such efficient digestive systems they do not need to poop. If a bear poops, they do it completely out of spite.

Bear diet research has revealed that bears often choose their sources of nourishment based on the benefits that different kinds of meat can have on their physiology. For instance, bears eat salmon because the fat in salmon helps to lubricate their joints to avoid arthritis. Likewise, bears eat crying humans because human tears provide much-needed salt that helps them retain water and store nutrients. Though research into the benefits that bears gain from eating a variety of proteins is ongoing, many fascinating discoveries have been made. Below are just some of the findings.

FOOD	BENEFITS (Unique to bears)
 **HONEY**	Because honey is made by bees, it possesses a nutrient that gives bears the ability to communicate telepathically, just like bees can. That is also why it tastes sweet to humans.
NINJA MEAT	Ninjas contain a small amount of shadow protein. Eaten in large doses, shadow protein will make a bear much better at hiding and performing stealth kills.
ANGEL WING MEAT	Bears commonly eat angels. The wing meat of angels aids bears in their ability to execute excellent aerial attacks like atomic elbows and body splashes.
DOG MEAT	Dogs give off a chemical that makes them desirable to humans. Bears eat dogs and gain this chemical so that humans foolishly think of bears as big cuddly dogs rather than roving hell-beasts.
LEPRECHAUNS	Leprechaun meat gives bears no nourishment, but due to ursine superstition, bears think eating it brings them good luck.

Bear droppings are extremely high in ninja protein.

Digestive System

Bears have a unique digestive system. Unlike other creatures who can only digest organic matter such as meat and vegetation, bears can also digest non-physical things like spirits, emotions, and religions. Thanks to this fascinating ability, bears are able to consume angels, demons, poltergeists, Satan, and other spirits, in addition to rabbits, blueberries, and hikers.

Bears Have Two Stomachs

And one for souls

One for meat

If you are eaten by a bear, you shall not pass on to the next world.

When a bear eats a living thing, it swallows both its physical body and its spirit. A bear has two stomachs for this process, one that processes organic matter and one that stores souls. The bear's second stomach contains an infinite realm known as "Beargatory," a place between life and death, where prey remains forever in eternal torment.

The soul of a bear victim lives in eternal torment all of their days in a realm known as Beargatory.

SLEEP HABITS

While bears don't sleep as long as we have been led to believe, when they do sleep, they have vivid, chaotic dreams about salmon and human suffering. Using new technology to collect snapshots from inside of a bear's mind while it is sleeping, many scientists have become traumatized and incapable of getting on with life. Imagery from bear dreams contained the following:

THINGS BEARS DREAM ABOUT

- Big juicy salmon

- A human being turned inside out

- Bleeding eye sockets

- Medieval torture devices

- Honey

- Babies with harlequin ichthyosis

- Atomic holocaust

- Weeping and gnashing of teeth

- People burning

- The lurking darkness within every human soul

- 73 new species of cockroach

- Blood. So much blood.

- Berries

Hibernation

You've probably heard the stories of how bears spend up to 7½ months sleeping in caves, somehow never urinating and muscles never atrophying. You probably thought that sounded a little crazy. That's because it was.

Hibernation is a myth that has lasted for centuries. In truth, when bears sneak off into caves for months on end, they are not hibernating. They are getting beasted up, pumping iron and getting mad jacked. The technical term for this period is "hibearnation."

It turns out that bears are nature's gym rats. They have extensive home weight sets with tons of dumbbells, barbells, and other weightlifting devices like hollowed-out rhinoceroses stuffed with civil war-era cannonballs, which they pump without ceasing for up to 7½ months every year. It's an impressive gym regimen and another reason they are probably going to wipe us out.

Humans can't compete with a bear's max reps and mad gains.

Researchers have had little luck entering bear gyms without being messed the hell up, but on the few occasions the isolated shred factories have been observed, they mostly contain free weights. "Bears think weight machines are for noobs and jabronies," observed one of the researchers. "They also go straight-up bitchcakes when some feather lifter doesn't wipe up their sweat. Do you even lift?"

Though the actual practice of bear weightlifting has not been well documented, the reason behind it is clear. Bears have one thing in mind: world domination. You can't force an entire planet to its knees if you aren't stacked like a beast.

REPRODUCTIVE SYSTEM

Unlike most species, bears do not reproduce using their genitals. Bears are *panmaphrodoxic*, possessing not just common male and female genitalia (which usually fall off in infancy), but a Swiss Army knife of reproductive organs completely unique to their species. Most of these are hidden inside of the bear's nether regions under a paunch of fur called the furnipaxis. These appendages and added organs give the bear a number of options when seeking to reproduce.

KNOWN BEAR REPRODUCTIVE ORGANS

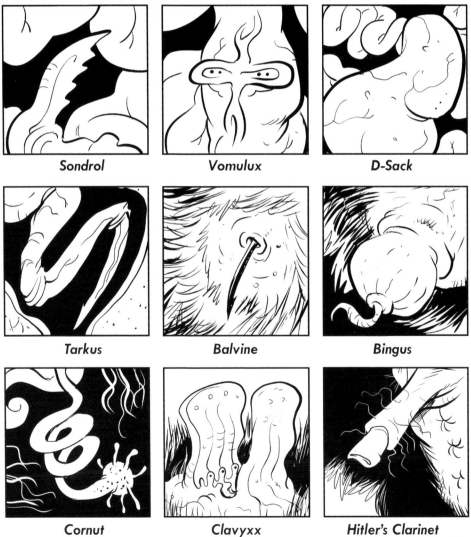

Sondrol   *Vomulux*   *D-Sack*

Tarkus   *Balvine*   *Bingus*

Cornut   *Clavyxx*   *Hitler's Clarinet*

Reproduction Methods

Below are just a small sampling of the ways a bear might create offspring.

The Sondrol

The sondrol is like a small saw-blade made of bone that sits on the spine like a propeller. If the bear wants to create an instant copy of itself, the sondrol will begin to spin and saw the bear into two pieces in a matter of seconds (Fig. A). Once the bear is rent asunder, the two halves will rapidly grow into two separate bears (Fig. B). These bears will be of two bodies but one mind.

Fig. A: *The spinning blade-like sondrol divides the bear into two pieces at the midsection.*

Fig. B: *The two halves of the bear regenerate like starfish, but at a rapid rate.*

Fig. C: *Within seconds, the bear has become two bears.*

Balvine and Tarkus

The tarkus is a long, spear-like appendage used to lay eggs. The balvine is like a barbed stinger. Much like the tarantula wasp, bears will seek out cow or bull elk, battle them, incapacitate them using the poison secretions of the balvine, then, penetrating their rib cage with the tarkus, lay eggs in their body. The animal will awaken hours later, believing it survived the encounter. Over the next couple of days, the creature will feel ill, getting constant headaches, dizziness, and burning stomach ulcers. Finally, following severe chest pains, a full-grown bear will burst from the animal's innards, killing it instantly, the miracle of life having taken its full course.

1. During fight, bear stings cow with balvine poison.

2. Bear uses tarkus to insert egg into unconcious cow.

3. Cow wakes up, unaware it is carrying bear larva.

4. Bear reaches maturation, emerges.

In one of life's greatest miracles, a brand new bear emerges from a host cow.

The Vomulux

If a bear needs to reproduce rapidly, it can do so by vomiting. An organ in its throat called the vomulux will disperse popcorn-kernel sized seeds into its throat which it will then vomit out with a mixture of reproductive excretions that cause rapid fertilization. Much like popcorn kernels on a hot stove, the seeds will burst rapidly into bears, creating a small ursine army within seconds.

1. Bear vomits kernels.

2. A bunch of bears suddenly pop up like popcorn.

The D-Sack

A bear has a sack inside its body near its inner right thigh that, when fully developed, acts as a defense mechanism if the animal comes into contact with an explosion. When a bear is bombed, it will burst into pieces and the D-sack (decimation sack) will burst, erupting a reproductive mist that will disperse among the disintegrated body parts, causing each individual bit to rapidly reconstruct into a separate bear. By the time each piece lands, it has become a new bear.

__IMPORTANT__: Bears do not explode. They burst into a million bears.

Nurturing of Young (The Cub Myth)

Despite common misconceptions, bears do not nurture their young. Bears are born full-sized.

"But wait," you might say. "What about bear cubs? I have seen those all over the nature channel and on YouTube."

It is true that bears can often be seen traveling with other, smaller bears in their company. These smaller bears are not actually separate bears. One full-sized bear can disperse into three or four sub-bears (what we call cubs). Sub-bears can disperse into even smaller sub-bears until they are microscopic. While there may be a limit to the number of sub-bears one bear can divide into, science has not found it. Bears can divide into millions, maybe even billions of sub-bears.

If a bear is in its sub-bear state (appearing as multiple small bears instead of one large bear), it is usually utilizing each individual sub-bear to sniff for scent trails, search for prey, and keep a lookout. The smaller the sub-bears, the easier it is for a bear to pass through small openings, such as keyholes and a human eye socket. It is estimated that the average human being has up to 1,700 microscopic sub-bears lurking inside them at any given time.

Despite what you might think, this is not a mother bear and cubs. This is one bear divided into three sub-bears: One 2/3 sub-bear and two 1/6 sub-bears.

SIZE AND WEIGHT

Bears range in size from microscopic to several times larger than the largest universe. Most people do not realize that they are in contact with bears all the time. They are in your plants, your mattresses, even the trunk of your car. There is strong evidence to suggest that the universe itself is simply a tiny speck of dust on the eyelash of an immense bear deity, who is a mere thought inside the brain of bear god the size of a billion multiverses.

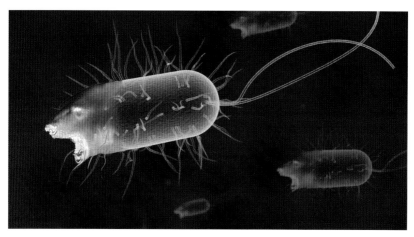

Electron microscope images of the Epstein-Bear Virus.

New scientific discoveries are being made daily as to the variety of bears in the known universe. This is because bears come in many forms. More information about the variety of bears will be found in ensuing chapters.

Planet Bearcury, the largest and hairiest planet in the known universe.

BEAR SIZE CATEGORIES

Micro-bears *(0.1 nanometer - 1mm)*

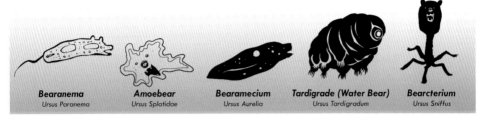

Bearanema
Ursus Paranema

Amoebear
Ursus Splatidae

Bearamecium
Ursus Aurelia

Tardigrade (Water Bear)
Ursus Tardigradum

Bearcterium
Ursus Sniffus

Aqua-bears *(0.1 nanometer - 1mm)*

Bear Trout
Ursus Salmo Trutta

Bearwhal
Ursus monodon monoceros

Octobear
Ursus Octopus Vulgaris

Bear Shark
Ursus Amblyrhynchos

Land Bears *(100 lbs. - 5,000 lbs.)*

Black Bear
Ursus Americanus

Grizzly Bear
Ursus Arctos Horribilis

Polar Bear
Ursus Maritimus

Bearnoceros
Ursus Rhinocerotidae

BEAR SIZE CATEGORIES
(continued)

Mega Bears *(10,000,000 - 5,000,000,000 tons)*

Bearantula
Ursus theraphosa blondi

Megabear
Ursus Seatopius

Bearzilla
Ursus Hondatanakus

King Gibearah
Ursus Garogaus

Bear gods and demigods *(1,000 - 10, 000,000, 000 metameters)*

Bearcano
Ursus Hotlavacus

Bearstroid
Ursus Meteorus Del Muerte

The Megatardigrade
Ursus Tardigrandeus

Chapter 2

Bear Habitats and Interactions With Nature Mostly Through Devastating Piledrivers

BEARS CAN LIVE ALMOST ANYWHERE and have long-lasting effects on the forests, ecosystems, cities, or planets where they have been present. Not only do bears shed a large amount of fur, leave deep scratch marks in most surfaces, and spray nearly everything they encounter with a pungent musk in order to assert territorial ownership, but they also attack everything in sight.

We will get into specific methods of attack in later chapters. In this chapter we will look at where bears live and how they use their surroundings for purposes of fight training, species dominance, food, and most of all, devastating piledrivers from death-insuring heights.

WHERE BEARS LIVE

Bears can live just about anywhere, though they prefer human living rooms, dens and master bedrooms the most. Below are some of the main places bears live.

On Land

This includes every continent of earth, and other planets.

This is an example of some land. Many bears live on land.

In the Arctic

Mass extinction has been a huge problem in the Arctic. When is the last time you heard about Eskimos? See, they're extinct, or at least heavily endangered thanks to polar bears, a predatory bear who can camouflage themselves in white to blend in with their surroundings. There has been a secret government initiative to melt icebergs to get rid of polar bears which has been highly ineffective and has only made them angrier.

The U.S. Government has put billions into global warming, hoping to melt the ice caps and get rid of polar bears. However, polar bears can swim, so this is a stupid plan.

In the Ocean

Other bears live in the ocean. The ocean is enormous, so it is not common for humans to catch a glimpse of sea bears (also known as bearmaids). Also, unlike sharks, bearmaids have no dorsal fin that exposes their position. And unlike the Kraken or Moby Dick, nobody ever survives a sea bear attack and lives to tell the tale. If you see one, you die.

These warnings do nothing to deter human aquatic activities because humans are fools.

In the Clouds

Sometimes you think you see the shape of a bear in the clouds but it's just an optical illusion. These can be nice moments. But other times it really is a cloud bear. If you see an actual cloud bear, you will die horribly.

Son : That cloud looks just like a bear, dad.
Dad: It is a bear you foolish child. (both die)

In Space

There is life on other planets, but it is only bears. The fact is, Earth is the last planet left in the ursine conquest of the universe. The reason there is no life on other planets is because bears already wiped it out.

There used to be lots of life on other planets, then bears showed up.

In You

Single-celled bears are a genus of unicellular ciliated protozoan, often found in stagnant basins and ponds, but also in bear pee, sweat, saliva, and sneezes. Once a human comes in contact the microscopic beast enters the blood stream. This bear devours humans one cell at a time.

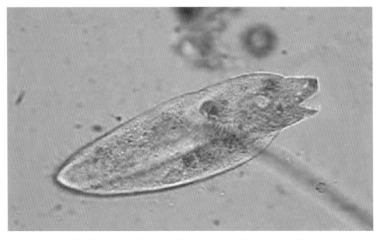

The bearamecium is the #1 cause of the Bear Flu.

HOW BEARS USE THEIR SURROUNDINGS

Attack Practice

Bears use their surroundings to develop and perfect their attacks. Whether they are clawing eagles out of the sky, felling trees with their hind legs, or surprising other woodland creatures with an RKO out of nowhere, bears use the terrain and various inhabitants of the forest as a fight-training obstacle course, all in preparation for their confrontations with humans, whether they be the common hiker or a trained military soldier.

The rich forest environment provides bears with an assortment of easy-to-take-down targets. Elk, which are very large, act as heavy punching bags. Salmon jumping upstream act as projectiles. Snakes can be stretched and used as a jump rope, or a double-ended striking bag if they have recently swallowed something large. Quail make great protien-heavy snacks.

Bears commonly practice moves such as a running clothesline on grazing elk.

Salmon Migration

The salmon migration is a great time for bears to practice striking. With the rapid, unpredictable movements of the jumping fish, bears have to think fast in order to knock the targets out of the air and onto the shore for later consumption.

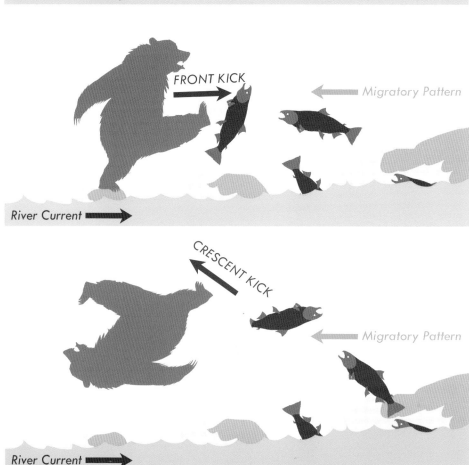

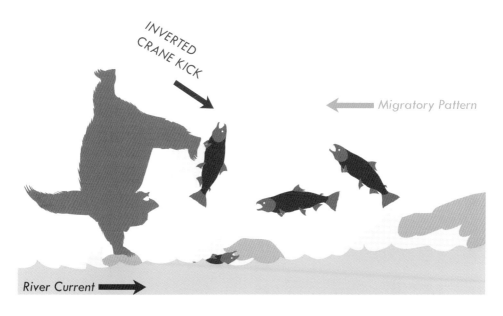

INVERTED CRANE KICK

Migratory Pattern

River Current

SPINNING ROUNDHOUSE KICK

Migratory Pattern

River Current

Did You Know?

Bears often surf the rapids on trees they've knocked over. This activity strengthens the animal's core, improves balance, and occasionally gives it the opportunity to clothseline thirsty forest animals who have come to the river bank for a drink.

Potential Clothesline Victim

River Current

The High Drive

Bears often use bluffs, cliff sides, waterfalls and other high points to perform attacks. Sometimes a bear will drag its prey for miles just to reach its preferred piledriving or elbow dropping elevation. If you are in bear country, steer clear of high points. Never go mountain climbing and never, ever visit waterfalls. Even out in the open you are unsafe if a bear in the area has a skydiving permit. Bears have been known to drop from airplanes and elbow drop unsuspecting victims out of nowhere.

This rare photo captures a grizzly bear piledriving a hiker off of a waterfall at Yosemite National Park.

Bears have been known to take several months of skydiving lessons just to be able to drop from planes to elbow drop their prey.

A hiking couple notices a bear majestically leaping from a cliff side to atomic elbow them.

THE PILEDRIVER

We will explore the wide variety of bear attacks in the coming pages, but it is important to isolate the bear's favorite finishing move. While some animals shake their jaws on the throat to finalize their kill, the bear prefers to turn them upside down and smash their skull beneath their hindquarters.

Many people think that the piledriver, a popular wrestling move in the WWF, WWE, WCW and other wrestling organizations, was created by men. In truth, the piledriver was invented by bears and is their favorite way to finish an attack. When humans perform the piledriver it is rarely fatal because they do not place their victim's head directly under their gluteus maximus. This is because human piledrivers are as fake as human wrestling.

When a bear does a piledriver, the mortality rate is 100%. No living thing survives a bear piledriver under any circumstance. The spine is shattered, the chest cavity crushed and the skull flattened under the weight of the bear's enormous buttocks. If the victim survives the smashing, the many diseases left on the injured victim from the dense, hellish bacteria in the bear's nether regions will eventually seal their fate.

STANDARD PILEDRIVER

FAKE

How a Bear Performs a Piledriver

Step 1: Once you are dazed, the bear will grab onto you.

Step 2: The bear flips you over in one swift movement.

Step 3: The bear will jump, often off a rock or branch.

Step 4: You are crushed beneath the bear's giant ass.

One of the only images capturing a bear performing a piledriver in its natural habitat.

WARNING: GRAPHIC CONTENT
This is an image of a bear piledriver victim. This is one of the few pile-driven corpses that did not burst into several pieces on impact.

BEARS VS. OTHER ANIMALS

There are many dangerous animals in the animal kingdom. Are bears really the most powerful? Extensive research pitting a bear against various species suggests that bears are not only a superior organism, but they fight dirtier and have spent more time inventing, practicing and using their fighting moves in real-life fights.

Bear vs. Elk

Fight time: *48 seconds*
Elk Attacks Executed: *Running away*
Damage done by Elk: *0*
Bear Attacks Executed: *Footsweep, spinning elbow, piledriver*
Damage Done by Bear: *100%*

Bear Wins by Piledriver

Bear vs. Golden Eagle

Fight time: *4.22 minutes*
Eagle Attacks Executed: *Talon swipe, retreat*
Damage done by Eagle: *None detected*
Bear Attacks Executed: *Double leg kick, chokeslam from top of tree, stomp, piledriver*
Damage Done by Bear: *100%*

Bear Wins by Piledriver

Bear vs. Wolf

Fight time: *37 seconds*
Wolf Attacks Executed: *One attempted bite*
Damage done by Wolf: *None detected*
Bear Attacks Executed: *Claw swipe, gut punch, knee to groin, piledriver*
Damage Done by Bear: *100%*

Bear Wins by Piledriver

Bear vs. Cougar

Fight time: *2.32 minutes*
Cougar Attacks Executed: *Clawing, biting*
Damage done by Cougar: *Minor scratches*
Bear Attacks Executed: *Claw swipe, half nelson, backhand slap, suplex, piledriver*
Damage Done by Bear: *100%*

Bear Wins by Piledriver

Bear vs. California Quail

Fight time: *.12 seconds*
Quail Attacks Executed: *None detected**
Damage done by Quail: *None detected*
Bear Attacks Executed: *Piledriver*
Damage Done by Bear: *100%*

Bear Wins by Piledriver

*There were rumors that a quail can fire a laser from its head plume but there was no evidence of this.

Bear vs. Great White Shark

Fight time: *5.36 minutes*
Shark Attacks Executed: *Bite, torpedo, tail whip*
Damage done by Shark: *12%*
Bear Attacks Executed: *Single knee face breaker, monkey flip, hip toss, chicken wing, Boston crab, piledriver*
Damage Done by Bear: *100%*

Bear Wins by Piledriver

Bear vs. Tiger

Fight time: *8.3 minutes*
Tiger Attacks Executed: *Claw swipe, bite*
Damage done by Tiger: *7%*
Bear Attacks Executed: *Corner back elbow, scissors kick, tiger feint kick, three-quarter face lock, arm-hook sleeper, piledriver*
Damage Done by Bear: *100%*

Bear Wins by Piledriver

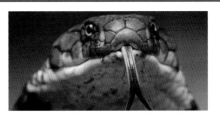

Bear vs. Cobra

Fight time: *3.03 minutes*
Cobra Attacks Executed: *Striking*
Damage done by Cobra: *Minor swelling*
Bear Attacks Executed:
Cannonball, flying lariat, Japanese arm drag, cobra clutch slam piledriver
Damage Done by Bear: *100%*

Bear Wins by Piledriver

Bear vs. Ninja

Fight time: *1.31 minutes*
Ninja Attacks Executed: *Half of one spinning roundhouse kick*
Damage done by Ninja: *None detected*
Bear Attacks Executed: *Dragonwhip, cactus clothesline, testicular claw, piledriver*
Damage Done by Bear: *100%*

Bear Wins by Piledriver

Bear vs. Racism

Fight time: *8.45 minutes*
Racism Attacks Executed: *Slurs, epithets, stereotypes*
Damage done by Racism: *8%*
Bear Attacks Executed: *Bear hug, diving head butt, moonsault, DDT, power bomb, piledriver*
Damage Done by Bear: *100%*

Bear Wins by Piledriver

Bear vs. Unicorn

Fight time: *12.07 minutes*
Unicorn Attacks Executed: *Poking, kicking, rainbow lasers, biting*
Damage done by Unicorn: *22%*
Bear Attacks Executed: *Hadou-coon, Frankensteiner, mouth laser, side suplex, battering ram, shining wizard, firebreather, piledriver*
Damage Done by Bear: *100%*

Bear Wins by Piledriver

Bear vs. Giraffe

Fight time: *0.3 minutes*
Giraffe Attacks Executed: *1 attempted head butt*
Damage done by Giraffe: *None detected*
Bear Attacks Executed: *Leg choke, throat thrust, slide sweep, piledriver**
Damage Done by Bear: *100%*

Bear Wins by Piledriver

*the research team did not take slow motion video of this, please stop emailing about it.

Bear vs. Silverback Gorilla

Fight time: *24 hours**

Gorilla Attacks Executed: *Head butt drop, forearm smash, spinning knee, elbow drop, vertical press, bionic elbow, sliding forearm smash, high knee, full nelson, pendulum, handspring, hair pull, cartwheel kick, quarter pounder, knee-meteor, spinning back hand, eye gouge, long knee, ax stomp, spinning bird kick, tiger uppercut, psycho crusher, banana peel, drill kick.*

Damage done by Gorilla: *Unknown*

Bear Attacks Executed: *Chop drop, tilt-a-whirl cross body, rebound clothesline, Mongolian chop, rapid claw swipe, back flip kick, calf kick, heart punch, eye poke, chair thrust, spinning uppercut, stink face, crescent kick, double elbow, spear-fish, throat punch, crash cymbal, nutcracker choke, fish hook, shippu jinrai kyaku, heel kick, bite, back-breaker, overhead, kick toss.*

Damage done by Bear: *Unknown*

The question of who would win in a fight between a silverback gorilla and a grizzly bear has plagued mankind for centuries. Further information on this mystery is in the afterword of this book.

**The research team only had enough funding to rent and insure the gorilla for 24 hours after which it had to be returned to its owner, Evander Holyfield.*

Further Research Needed

Chapter 3
Basic Bear Attacks

IT WOULD BE IMPOSSIBLE to record every bear attack technique in one book. Bear attacks are as numerous as the grains of sand on the seashore. Bears are experimental creatures. One of the reasons a bear is so likely to attack you is because it has been pondering a new attack method and wants to try it out on the nearest living thing. A bear never attacks the same way twice.

Some bear attacks get more use than others. There are a number of attacks that bears have been using for centuries to weaken their victims and to finish them off. As mentioned before, the piledriver is the bear's favorite way to end a fight.

In this section, we will look at the most basic bear attacks. These are the moves a bear is most likely to use on you if you encounter one in the wild. As you read, it will become obvious to you that all martial arts are but a shadow of the basic bear-fighting techniques that preceded mankind for ages.

CLAW ATTACKS

A bear's most standard attack comes from its claws. Let's take a closer look at these deadly weapons that every bear is born with in great abundance.

A Mitten Made of Steak Knives

A bear's claws are its most basic weapon. Like five steak knives sticking out of a furry mitten, a bear's claws are not just deadly because they cut through flesh like air, but because bears use them so effectively. Even the padding on a bear paw is full of death. A palm reader once tried to read the creases in the pad of a bear's palm and has not left the mental hospital since that day.

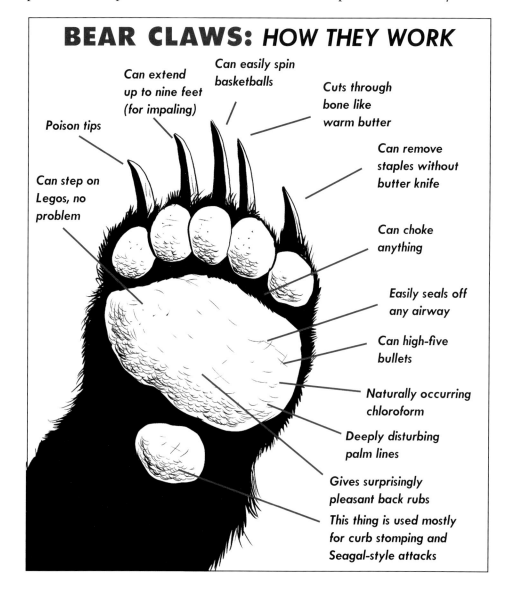

BEAR CLAWS: *HOW THEY WORK*

Can easily spin basketballs

Can extend up to nine feet (for impaling)

Cuts through bone like warm butter

Poison tips

Can remove staples without butter knife

Can step on Legos, no problem

Can choke anything

Easily seals off any airway

Can high-five bullets

Naturally occurring chloroform

Deeply disturbing palm lines

Gives surprisingly pleasant back rubs

This thing is used mostly for curb stomping and Seagal-style attacks

Basic Claw Attacks

Basic Face Claw

Advanced Face Claw

Tip of the Spear

Scissor Claw

Basic Claw Attacks (cont.)

Ice Cream
Scoop

Confetti
Style

The Clapper

Clawnado

BITING ATTACKS

A Meaty Hole Full of More Steak Knives

A bear's mouth is its other not-so-secret weapon. Though its tongue and gums are sensitive, the bear's mouth is filled with teeth, like a meaty hole full of hard-bone railroad spikes or steak knives made from bone. A bear can crush anything with its strong jaws, and there is nothing its powerful teeth cannot penetrate, including metal, steel, iron, scrap metal, heavy metal, death metal, and even chrome steel. A bear can even bite into non-physical matter like ghosts of the deceased, angel messengers, and self-esteem.

If you see this and it's not a photograph, you are probably about to die.

BEAR MOUTHS:
HOW THEY WORK

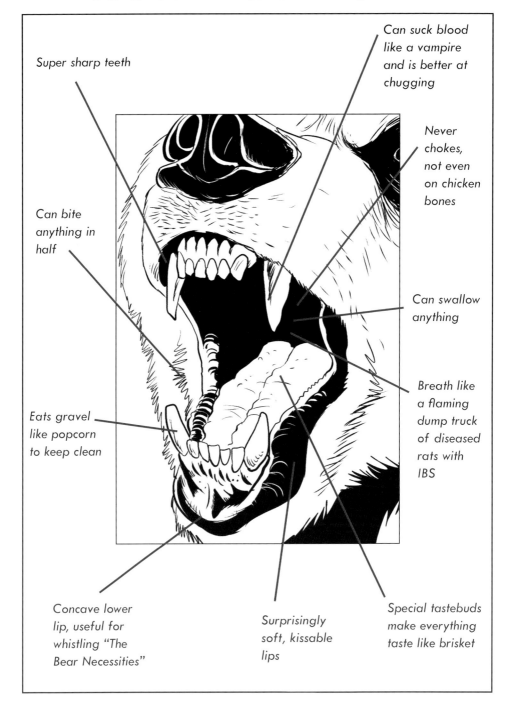

Can suck blood like a vampire and is better at chugging

Super sharp teeth

Never chokes, not even on chicken bones

Can bite anything in half

Can swallow anything

Eats gravel like popcorn to keep clean

Breath like a flaming dump truck of diseased rats with IBS

Concave lower lip, useful for whistling "The Bear Necessities"

Surprisingly soft, kissable lips

Special tastebuds make everything taste like brisket

Basic Bite Attacks

Basic Face Bite

Head Snack

Brain Spit

Muppet Swallow

Basic Bite Attacks (cont.)

Acid Spit

Essence Suck

Breath of Death

Tongue Slap

BEAR HUG ATTACKS

A Deadly Passion

There is nothing more passionate or deadly than a bear hug. The moment you find yourself in the embrace of a grizzly's front paws, you will never feel so loved or so asphyxiated as you do in that moment right before you die. The hug is the most efficient and unique form of bear attack.

(Left) A bear hug from the front is customary and usually results in a collapsed rib cage.

(Below) A bear hug from behind is considered more intimate and generally turns the victim's spine into tapioca pudding.

BEAR HUGS: *HOW THEY WORK*

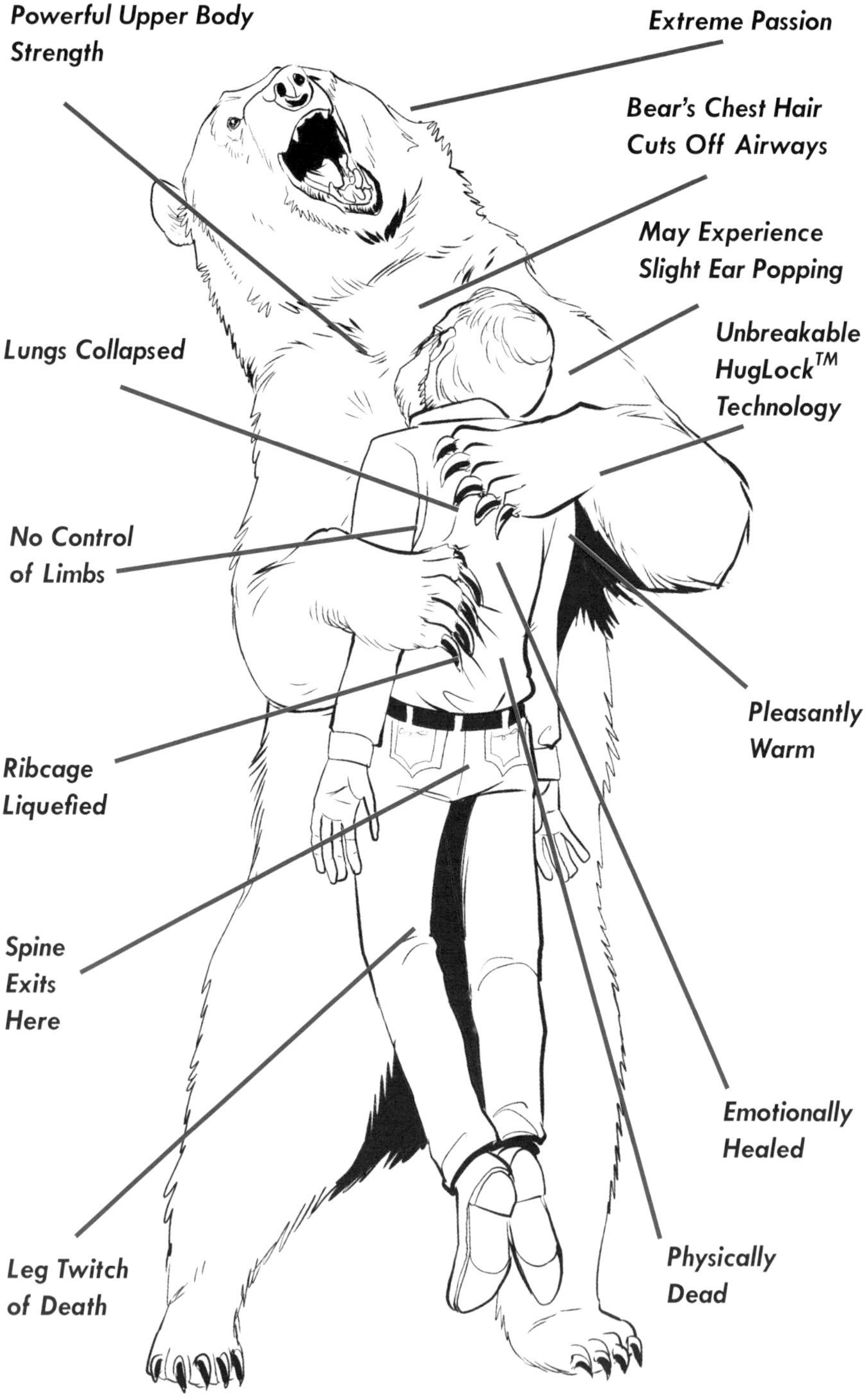

Powerful Upper Body
Strength

Extreme Passion

Bear's Chest Hair
Cuts Off Airways

May Experience
Slight Ear Popping

Lungs Collapsed

Unbreakable
HugLock™
Technology

No Control
of Limbs

Pleasantly
Warm

Ribcage
Liquefied

Spine
Exits
Here

Emotionally
Healed

Leg Twitch
of Death

Physically
Dead

Basic Hug Attacks

Basic Bro Hug

Extreme Bear Hug

The Twirl

Hug in the Rain

Basic Hug Attacks (cont.)

The Toothpaste Tube

The Boner

Topper Popper

Cry It Out

HOW A BEAR CAN CRUSH YOUR SOUL

While humans are capable of crushing each other's souls in a metaphorical sense, bears are capable of literally crushing souls.

1. *Bear hugs you to death, evacuating your soul.*

2. *Bear catches the tail of your soul before it floats to the afterlife.*

3. *Bear hugs your soul, crushing it to death.*

4. *Bear kicks your dead body and soul into the river.*

BEAR KICK ATTACKS

Bears possess extremely powerful legs. If a bear is on all fours and you approach it from behind, it will kick you just like a donkey. The only difference is that with a donkey, you will suffer moderate to severe injuries. With a bear, you will explode into multiple severed body parts upon impact.

Bears are masters of every kind of kick, from standard front kicks to jumping spin kicks, fly kicks, scissor kicks, roundhouse kicks, and crane kicks.

BEAR KICKS: *HOW THEY WORK*

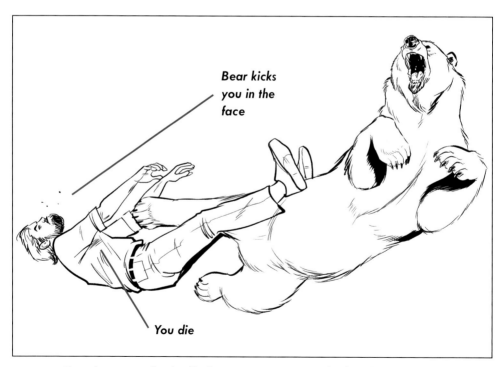

Bear kicks you in the face

You die

Bears have many levels of kicking power, starting at death and increasing to more extreme death involving dismemberment and exploding.

Bear Kicks: the Science

The hind legs of a bear can launch a force three million times their bodyweight. The sheer power is so extreme, the oxygen around the bear's leg turns to electricity and is ignited by the sudden rise in heat. An explosion occurs that follows the force of the leg through the victim, turning it into a cloudy mist of body parts, bone fragments, and death dust.

HOW EXPLODING BEAR KICKS WORK

Bear's lateral extensor muscle contracts then blasts forward with the power of an atomic jackhammer

The force causes oxygen around the paw to implode, creating an electricity tornado

Victim explodes on impact

A bear at the water's edge explodes a deer with a fierce rear kick.

Basic Kick Attacks

Front Kick

Fly Kick

Scissor Kick

Butterfly Kick

Did You Know?

Bears strengthen their legs by punting deer up to distances of over 320 yards. (That's two and a half football fields!)

Mule Kick
(aka the Ass Kicker)

Bicycle Kick

**Spinning Bear
Kick**

**Yippee-Ki-Yay
Mother Russia Kick**

**Naturally
Occuring Rocket
Leg Kick**
(used on hawks
and eagles)

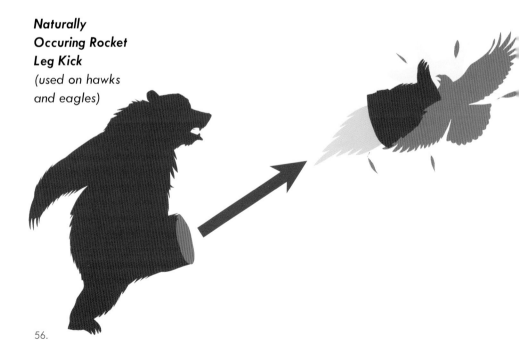

BODY/REAR END ATTACKS

Bears do not only utilize their claws and teeth in attacks. Bears often use the weight of their entire body to crush their prey. These aggressive creatures love jumping from high places to inflict maximum damage. Whether the end result is a belly splash, a butt drop, or a back flop, the outcome is always the same. The bear leaves a grease stain on the earth where its target once stood.

Sometimes when you hike through canyons, bears will body-splash you from the top of cliffs. The man in the above photograph did not survive this encounter.

Bears also like to do triple-half-gainers off the top of skyscrapers. This photograph was found in a camera next to a grease stain in downtown Manhattan.

One of the most unsafe places on Earth is within 10-20 feet of any tree. Photos like this are all too common as the last image on the camera of a flattened nature photographer.

DROP BEARS

While we are on the topic of bears dropping from the sky, it would be careless not to address the topic of the Australian "drop bear." According to Wikipedia, a drop bear is "...a predatory, carnivorous version of the koala (*Phascolarctos cinereus*). While koalas are typically docile herbivores... drop bears are described as unusually large and vicious marsupials that inhabit treetops and attack unsuspecting people (or other prey) that walk beneath them by dropping onto their heads from above."

Some believe the drop bear to be a hoax. Others claim that the only reason there isn't more published science on drop bears is because anyone who attempts research is mauled to death.

Apparent photograph of a real drop bear, though some photo-forensic experts claim it is fake.

Whether or not the Australian drop bear is real cannot be confirmed, but one thing is for sure: Koalas are not bears. Out of a deep sense of insecurity, koalas have attempted to use the bear moniker to portray something other than what koalas actually are: glorified sloths. If koalas were ever to attempt to take over the world (as bears absolutely are), natural entropy would win out first.

Many speculate that the drop-bear phenomenon was created by koalas as part of their campaign to emulate real bears like grizzlies, black bears, and Eurasian brown bears. While it is not commonly known that bears love dropping onto people and other animals from great heights, koalas, who are obsessive bear wanna-bes by nature, would know this and have every motivation to perpetuate such a myth.

This is the aftermath of a real-life drop bear attack.

Did You Know?

It is common knowledge that when a bear lands on a human being hindquarters-first, the person's body is smashed into a nearly unrecognizable puddle of mush.

But what makes this pile of mush so putrid is because at the point of impact — just milliseconds before the body is smashed beyond all recognition — the victim will instantly release all digestive waste from every orifice possible. Experts have dubbed this phenomenon "death sprinkler syndrome."

Basic Drop Attacks

*Belly
Splash*

*Back
Splash*

Butt Splash

*The Balloo
Splash*

Basic Drop Attacks (cont.)

Moonsault

Egyptian Splits

Atomic Elbow

*Dive
Bomber*

*Chillsville
Bomber*

*Diving
Clothesline*

AERIAL SLAMS AND DRIVERS

Sometimes a bear will take their victim to the edge of a cliff or the roof of a building to perform an aerial attack that requires dropping from a great height, with the victim in a position to experience various amounts of extreme damage. The piledriver is just one example of a move like this.

While a bear may perform any of these moves on level ground, they usually prefer to do them from a great height.

This bear is performing a superplex from the edge of a cliff.

Did You Know?

One of the biggest limitations on mankind's attempt to explore the universe is that bears nearly always stow away on rocket ships so they they can perform aerial moves on astronauts from outer space.

While most animals attempting an aerial reverse Frankensteiner in outer space would implode, bears can create gravity, do not require oxygen, and possess naturally occurring shoulder-blade jet packs, enabling them to plummet from any point in the galaxy to their chosen point of impact on the Earth's surface.

Aerial Slams and Drivers

**Upside-Down
Armlock
Back Slam**

**Inverted
Diving Gorilla
Press**

Backbreaker

*Common
Piledriver*

Aerial Slams and Drivers (cont.)

Fireman's Carry Slam

The Pogo Stomp

DDT

Slam Dunk

DASH ATTACKS

Bears are some of the fastest land animals on the planet. They use their lightness of foot and heavy frame to inflict impressive amounts of damage on anyone who may be in their way. Bears love performing various attacks while mid-run, including clotheslines, leg sweeps, and double-leg kicks.

If you like running, you should never run anywhere near the forest. Bears target runners with sweeps and clotheslines, and are rarely seen until they rock your jaw out of nowhere.

This jogger had no idea she was about to be clotheslined until it was too late.

Basic Dash Attacks

Running Clothesline

Running Face Kick

Slide Trip

The Thai Fighter

The Rama-Lama-Ding-Dong

**Double
Drop Kick**

*Running Chest
Bump*

The Harmadillo

Chapter 4
Advanced Bear Attacks

WE'VE HARDLY SCRATCHED THE SURFACE on basic bear attacks, but it's time to move on. Bears also perform advanced attacks that take them years to master. Many of these attacks harness cosmic energy, chemical reactions, satanic mysticism, friction, the dark arts, xi, ghosts, and other mysterious and metaphysical forces humans know little about, like magnets. Some of these attacks require intense amounts of time and planning, researching and learning human technology. Others are incredibly specific in their execution, like assembling a desk from IKEA. What binds together this subset of attacks is that they all take time to master or execute, are extremely dangerous, and are less common than the basic attacks in the previous chapter.

Once again, this is by no means an exhaustive listing of advanced bear attacks, only some of the most notable in various categories.

FIREBALL AND ENERGY ATTACKS

Bears have been working on harnessing natural and mystical energy for centuries. While a new bear can perform piledrivers and DDTs to kill you from the moment of conception, it takes ample time to learn to focus their xi, get in touch with the spirit world, and learn to harness organic energy to produce fireballs that can ultra-extra-super-kill you.

In a lush meadow, an older bear trains a newer bear how to harness energy into a fireball attack.

Bear attacks of this nature come in many varieties. Some bears can absorb lightning bolts and store them for later, shooting bolts of electricity from their mouths. Other times, bears will harness the life force of another animal and turn it into a projectile ball of otherworldly energy. Bears can harness any element — wind, fire, love, happiness, zinc — and weaponize it with proper time and training.

Did You Know?

Bears can use an entire flock of geese to send a flying V fireball attack south for the winter? Wherever the geese had intended to land on their journey toward warmth, the goose energy balls will home in on it and destroy it.

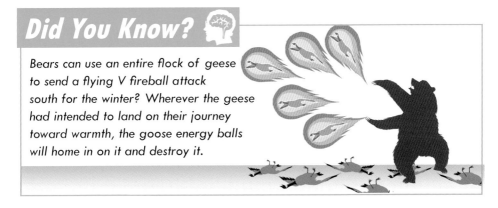

Bears may allow humans to put them into captivity, but only until they have mastered their fireball attacks.

Often, bears will allow themselves to be taken into captivity by humans. In zoos, circuses, and other institutions, bears are provided free room and board so that they can focus on energy-attack and fireball training with a variety of available targets. Once the animals have mastered this mysterious art, they will use it to decimate their surroundings and escape back into the wild. This is why zoos so often hold fundraisers.

If a bear targets you with one of these attacks, your chances of survival are zero to -1 billion, meaning that the best case scenario is you die, but you are much more likely to be launched into a metaphysical eternal realm of torture and sorrow that is far worse than death.

Here a bear absorbs the life force of a small shetland sheepdog.

Fireball and Energy Attacks

Salmon Storm

▲ Summoning the souls of the last 1,000+ salmon the bear ate yesterday, it fires the gilled ghosts at the enemy in an overwhelming blitzkrieg attack.

Devil Loogie

▲ Sometimes a bear will hock a loogie at you that turns out to literally be Satan.

74.

Hadou-coon

▲ Absorbing the soul of a nearby raccoon, the bear creates a projectile fireball attack that travels up to 5 miles an hour.

Lightning Belch

▲ After drinking a lake that was struck by lightning, a bear will let forth a belch of thunderbolts, tazing entire countrysides to death.

Fireball and Energy Attacks (cont.)

Ghost Impaler

▲ *After you are killed, the bear will impale your ghost as it tries to float away with a giant laser sword from its chest, robbing you of both life and afterlife.*

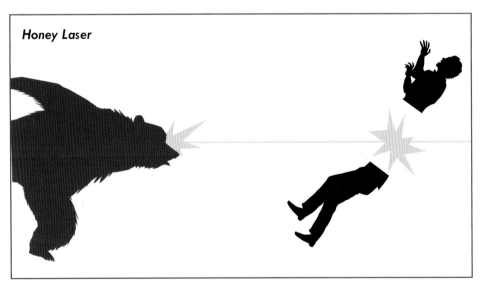

Honey Laser

▲ *After enough honey has been consumed, the bear will focus the honey's potent sweetness into a thin and very lethal laser that can cut through anything instantly.*

Roar-nado

▲ *Pretty self-explanatory. The bear roars out a tornado made of spirits, lasers, and fire that tears your flesh off your bones, the roof off your house, and causes multiple devastating tsunamis in various countries, ultimately depositing your corpse in Munchkinland.*

Fecal Murder

▲ *Channeling the tortured souls of every living thing the bear has ever consumed, it emits a hybrid spirit-ghost-hell monster from the opening in its anal region that wreaks havoc for centuries.*

ENVIRONMENT-SPECIFIC ATTACKS

While bears can inflict plenty of damage no matter where they are by using the strength, teeth, and claws given to them by Mother Nature, bears also like to find creative ways to use their surroundings to do harm in new and uncommon ways.

One of the main reasons bears travel to different continents and climates is to learn the environment and come up with ways to attack people using what is available to them in any given context. Whether they are waiting in a swamp to pull you into the mire, or hiding in the back of your car with a plastic bag to put over your head, bears can use any environment to put a new spin on murder.

Always check your back seat for grizzly bears.

Environment-Specific Attacks

Sioux-Plex

▲ *This move can only be performed in Sioux Falls, South Dakota. The bear takes its victim to the top of one of the falls and suplexes them off of it. Bears will often travel hundreds of miles, dragging a victim to perform this move.*

Did You Know?

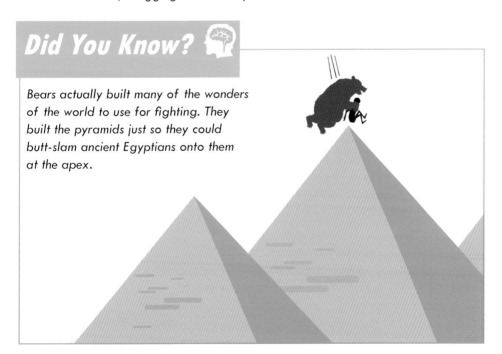

Bears actually built many of the wonders of the world to use for fighting. They built the pyramids just so they could butt-slam ancient Egyptians onto them at the apex.

Environment-Specific Attacks (cont.)

Shopping Bag

▲ The bear buys something inexpensive at a shopping mall so that it can acquire a plastic bag, then hides in the back of a car in the parking garage and waits for someone to get into the driver's seat so that it can suffocate them using the plastic bag. This is one reason you should never leave plastic laying around in the forest.

Ice Sculpture

▲ In colder climates, a bear will create intricate ice sculptures to attract tourism, then when the area is full of people, punch the sculpture so that everyone is impaled by sharp pieces of ice.

Lava Boarding

▲ A bear will use a human being as a surfboard to ride waves of hot lava until the person has disintegrated in the heat. Bears compete to see who can last the longest, and will often activate volcanoes just to practice this highly specialized sport.

Elepinata

▲ On occasions when a bear is feeling particularly vicious, the relentless animal will go to Asia and capture an elephant, then drag it to Mexico, hollow it out, then turn it into a pinata full of screaming human beings. It will then beat it to pieces with a board.

SECRET ATTACKS

A secret attack is a bear attack that goes under the radar of other living things. The victims and witnesses never knew that a bear was involved. Usually the attack may be blamed on something besides bears, such as air pollution or high-salt diets.

Throughout history, many disasters have been secret bear attacks. Many of the fires in southern California are not man-made but bear-made. The presidency of Jimmy Carter was almost all orchestrated by bears, as well as a majority of the American economic recessions. Bears infected birds with toxins so that they would be blamed for the bird flu. In the Garden of Eden, it was a bear using a sock puppet that caused the fall of mankind. Even the early cancellation of *Firefly*, and the sixth season of *24* were caused by bears.

A bear sneaks off after causing a flood that would end up being blamed on a dam failure.

Secret Attacks

Dam Failures

▲Often, in order to practice surfing, bears will destroy dams so that they can simultaneously catch waves and devastate forests and civilized populations. No dam failure has ever been blamed on a bear, though many remain suspect, especially those in areas rich in salmon and honey.

Did You Know?

Most dietary restrictions are false, and the number one cause of the obesity epidemic is bears. Often the likeliness that a food will cause you to be murdered by bears is right there on the label, but few people know to even look for it.

ALWAYS CHECK THE LABEL!

Nutrition Facts/Datos de Nutrición

8 servings per container/8 raciónes por envase
Serving size/Tamaño por ración — 1 cup / 1 taza (68g)

Amount per serving / Cantidad por ración

Calories / Calorias — **370**

	% Daily Value*/Valor Diario*
Total Fat/Grasa Total 5g	**7%**
Saturated Fat/Grasa Saturada 1g	**5%**
Trans Fat/Grasa *Trans* 0g	
Cholesterol/Colesterol 0mg	**0%**
Sodium/Sodio 150mg	**6%**
Total Carbohydrate/Carbohidrato Total 48g	**15%**
Dietary Fiber/Fibra Dietética 5g	**14%**
Total Sugars/Azúcares Total 13g	
Includes 10g Added Sugars/Incluye 10g azúcares añadidos	**20%**
Protein/Proteínas 12g	
Bear Murder Likeliness extreme	**-100%**
Vitamin D/Vitamina D 2mcg	10%
Calcium/Calcio 210mg	20%
Zinc 7mg	50%
Biotin/Biotina 300mcg	100%

* The % Daily Value (DV) tells you how much a nutrient in a serving of food contributes to a daily diet. 2,000 calories a day is used for general nutrition advice.
* El % Valor Diario (VD) le indica cuánto un nutriente en una porción de alimentos contribuye a una dieta diaria. 2,000 calorías al día se utiliza para asesoramiento de nutrición general.

Derailments

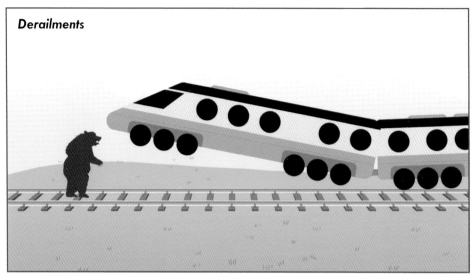

▲ Bears often run down train tracks playing chicken with oncoming locomotives. Since bears are never chicken, and because trains cannot avoid head-on collisions, the outcome is always a train being derailed.

Salt Assault

▲ Bears will often stealth kill someone who eats a large amount of salt, so that the health industry will mistakenly blame salt for the person's death. Bears possess the ability to detect high levels of salt by using their sense of smell. Once they find a salty victim, they kill them. Even if you avoid salt, bears still win because you will die from the misery of living a life of eating bland food.

Traffic Pile-ups

▲ It is common for bears to practice their foot sweeps on speeding cars and trucks. A bear will slide onto a freeway, trip one car, and cause a massive pileup, but bears rarely get the blame for this kind of disaster.

Old Age

▲ Sometimes death is blamed on old age, but it's actually bears — they always get you in the end, even if they have to wait until you're just too old to outrun them. Bears aren't above body-slamming the elderly.

GROUP ATTACKS

While bears are not particularly cooperative, they do operate from a hive mind. In fact, since many bears are simply copies of the same bear (especially when traveling in sleuths), when they attack as a group, they often act in perfect harmony with one another.

When bears come together to combine power, their attacks can be devastating. *The Care Bears*, a popular cartoon the the 1980s, drew from this fact with the "Care-Bear-Stare", a fictional version of a real attack in which bears line up and aim their inner energy field collectively in one direction. The truth behind this attack is that it's anything but caring. When bears jointly focus their power on one object, group, or city, the results are complete destruction.

Top: Four bears on a cliffside overlooking a forest perform a "stare."
Bottom: *The results.*

Group Attacks

The Spike

▲ In the move that inspired volleyball, one bear kicks the head off the neck, the next spikes the head, then a third bear catches it in its mouth.

The Neptune Strangler

▲ This is a planetary attack where bears form a single-file line around a planet, creating a tight ring, then lock arms and squeeze, "choking" the planet out.

See You Next Fall

▲ One bear crouches behind you while the other shoves you over him. Though this attack is not deadly, it will devastate your feelings.

MASS EXTINCTION ATTACKS

While bears are capable of wiping out large numbers of people at a time, they don't do this very often because—at least for now—they are using people as disposable punching bags and walking snacks. If bears want to wipe out thousands of people at one time, they have many tricks up their proverbial sleeves.

Above is an actual photograph of a bearsplosion that wiped out seven city blocks.

In the rare instances when bears have wiped out entire towns, government officials have swooped in to cover up the incident and either wipe the existence of the people or places involved out of public record, or to fabricate an alternative story blaming either Mother Nature or hostile enemies of the state. Our government rightly believes that most people could not emotionally handle the truth about how destructive bears really are, therefore they feel forced to lie about bear attacks to maintain public morale.

In this newspaper clipping, evidence is reported of the government covering up a town that was destroyed by bears.

Mass Extinction Attacks

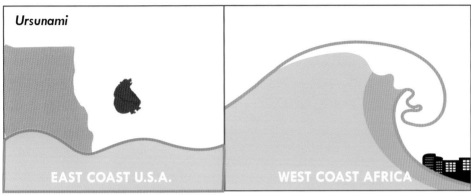

Ursunami

EAST COAST U.S.A.

WEST COAST AFRICA

▲ When a bear does cannonballs into the sea on one continent, this happens on the next.

Bruce Killis

▲ If bears sense extinction-level asteroids are heading toward Earth, they will kill Bruce Willis so nothing can stop it. Ben Affleck will be left unharmed.

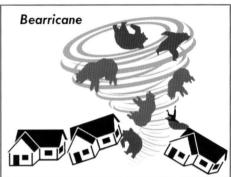

Bearricane

▲ A bearricane is 1,000 times more devastating than a sharknado.

This bearricane wiped the coast of Utah off the map. Now Utah is no longer a coastal state.

CYBERBULLYING AND ATTACKS ON SOCIAL MEDIA

This man escaped a bear attack while hiking, but when he returned, the attacks only got more intense online.

Even if you manage to avoid bears while you are outdoors, the chances of being attacked by bears online remains very high.

Bear Attacks Often Continue on Social Media

Many who claim to have survived bear attacks find that the attacks continue on social media long after the actual physical encounter. Though it is possible to block and report bear accounts, bears will relentlessly create new accounts to continue the online assault. If you are being harassed by a bear on social media, the best thing you can do is give up on technology altogether.

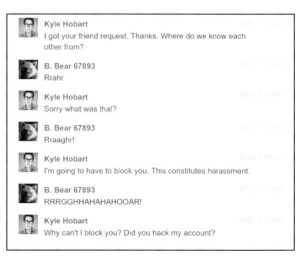

Never direct message a bear, or accept a friend request from one.

Bear Hackers

Bears frequent coffee shops and libraries, or anywhere else with a shared public WiFi connection. Bears are extremely strong animals and can tear easily through most firewalls, and they often know your password before you come up with it.

Bear hackers often hang out in coffee shops.

That next free program you install might include a bear attack.

Spyware

Have you ever downloaded free software that seemed too good to be true? Often, during the installation process, software companies will leave boxes pre-checked that invite bear attacks. It's up to you to deselect the box marked "I Agree" next to the cumbersome end-user license agreement (aka End Life by Bears Agreement) that includes consent to have your address sent to bears and your flesh eaten by them. Next time you think you've found free software, read the small print.

Facebook Groups

Sometimes you log onto Facebook only to realize you've been added to a group you never joined. It turns out anyone can add you to their group without your permission. Check the groups you've been added to and you just might find you were placed in a "Bears, Go Ahead and Kill Me," group without your consent. While Facebook gives you the option in your account settings to not allow people to add you to groups without you accepting, they still haven't installed this setting for bears, leaving all users open to attack.

Bears can add you to their group without your consent.

FATALITIES

While it is true that many bear attack moves could be considered "fatalities" in the sense that the attack in an instant kill, there are specific moves designed by bears to end a victim's life in a flashy, climactic finale of blood and guts. The popular *Mortal Kombat* videogame franchise from the 1990s mimicked many bear fatalities, though they toned them down to be more suitable for a family audience.

WARNING: THIS PORTION OF THE BOOK CONTAINS GRAPHIC AND OFTEN DISTURBING MATERIAL THAT WILL GIVE YOU NIGHTMARES FOR THE REST OF YOUR LIFE.

As part of its final, fatal attack, this bear has ripped out a man's spleen and is displaying it proudly in a kung fu stance.

Did You Know?

Bears will often utilize ancient healing techniques or stolen hospital equipment to resuscitate their victims in order to perform multiple fatalities.

Fatalities

Spirit Bear

▲ Unlike the myth perpetuated by Native Americans and the Walt Disney Corporation, when a bear spirit enters your body, you explode.

Man Shirt

▲ Bear puts you on like a shirt, then does a human impression to make friends laugh.

NBA Jam

▲ Bear slamdunks your head so hard, it starts on fire and the backboard breaks.

That's Amore

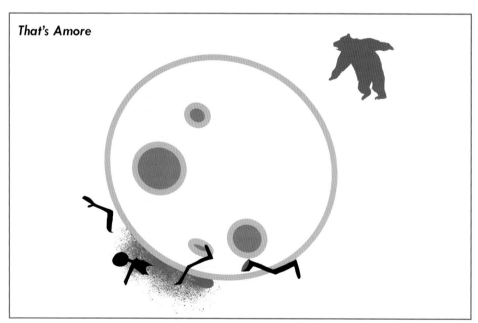

▲ When the moon hits your eye and you explode and die.

Chapter 5
How to Be Prepared

THERE ARE ALREADY MANY texts written about how to be prepared for a bear attack. Most of these rest on the false presumption that, with the proper preparation, you can avoid or even stop a bear attack. This is a comforting lie people pay money to be told. The truth we all must face is that there is no stopping bears from killing you.

Prepare to Die

The most important thing to remember when preparing for bear attacks is that you are preparing to die. Don't mess around with any other contingency plan. Planning to survive a bear attack is like planning to have a civil discussion on Twitter. It's unrealistic. Instead of thinking about trying to survive, think about how you want to die. Go for a glorious bear death; don't just be another clothesline victim.

MAN-MADE "BEAR TRAPS"

It's important to dispell the myth of bear traps. These rustic wall decorations are like the dream catchers of the early settler. Neither catches what they claim to catch; they are simply there for purposes of fantasy and wishful thinking. Bears cannot be stopped by what amounts to a metal puppet that bites onto their leg. Bears can easily chew their own leg off and grow a new one.

Are there any traps that work on bears?

No.

Bear traps are a great novelty item to hang in your cabin and nothing more.

BEAR TRAPS WHY THEY DON'T WORK

1. Bear gets paw caught in trap.

2. Bear gnaws off paw.

2. Bear regenerates improved limb of its choosing (just a few examples below.)

Mantis Claw   **Insane Clown Hammer**   **Infinite Gatling Gun**

Real Bear Traps

True bear traps are not made for bears by humans but vice versa. Bears are master trap setters. Bears rarely set live traps. Almost all are lethal. If a bear sets a live trap, they have plans for you beyond your worst nightmares. If there was a way to spot or avoid bear traps, this book would contain that information, but the current knowledge on bear traps is simply that you don't know you're in one until it's too late. Even this book could be a bear trap.

Bears are excellent trappers and often trade human skin and hair as currency.

Did You Know?

Similar to the way humans use cheese to coax mice into mouse traps, bears use a variety of bait to entice humans. Here some example of bait used by bears to trap humans.

COMMON BAIT USED BY BEARS

Pudding

Cuban Cigars

Suitcase of Money

Nachos

Corporate Success

Inflatable Woman

Free Water Slide

Examples of Bear Traps

Beer and Boulder

▲ In this classic trap, a beer is placed under a boulder balanced on a stick. When the beer is sought out, the bear tugs a rope attached to the stick, crushing the victim.

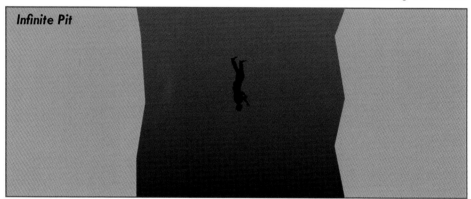

Infinite Pit

▲ In this trap, a pit is dug to infinity then covered with grass. When it is stepped onto, the victim falls and falls for all of eternity.

Hot Mamma Bear

▲ Sometimes a bear will dress up as an attractive woman only to trap you in a loveless marriage that will last decades and end violently.

SITUATIONS TO AVOID

Part of avoiding bear attacks is being aware that there are situations you can avoid that are almost guaranteed to attract a bear attack. Here are some of the top situations you should stay clear of.

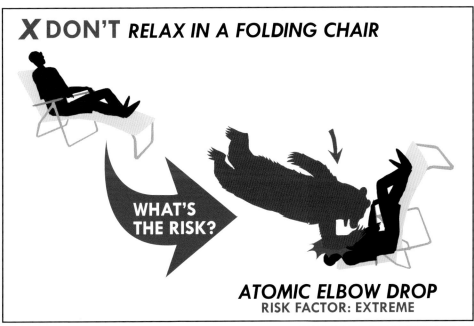

X DON'T *RELAX IN A FOLDING CHAIR*

WHAT'S THE RISK?

ATOMIC ELBOW DROP
RISK FACTOR: EXTREME

X DON'T *BEND OVER TO PICK UP KEYS*

WHAT'S THE RISK?

SIDE SUPLEX
RISK FACTOR: EXTREME

✗ DON'T *STAND BY A GLASS COFFEE TABLE*

WHAT'S THE RISK?

POWER BOMB
RISK FACTOR: EXTREME

✗ DON'T *SLEEP ON OPEN FLOOR AREA*

WHAT'S THE RISK?

REVERSE ELBOW SLAM
RISK FACTOR: EXTREME

X DON'T *TRY NOT TO VOMIT*

WHAT'S THE RISK?

DDT
RISK FACTOR: EXTREME

X DON'T *CLIMB TURNBUCKLE*

WHAT'S THE RISK?

FRANKESTEINER
RISK FACTOR: EXTREME

X DON'T *ATTEMPT TO RUN AWAY*

WHAT'S THE RISK?

RUNNING CLOTHESLINE
RISK FACTOR: EXTREME

X DON'T *GO TO THE POLICE*

WHAT'S THE RISK?

DOUBLE PILEDRIVER
RISK FACTOR: EXTREME

PROPER FOOD STORAGE

All food attracts bears. The moment you even think about having your next meal you are at risk of giving away your position to bears. While the smartest course of action is to simply never eat again (also known as the super model method), if you must eat, here are some basic guidelines.

Bears see human refrigerators as high-tech doggy-bags, free for the taking.

Food Product	Consumption Guidelines	Preparation Recommendations	Storage	Bear Appetite Rating
Meats	Devour immediately from live animal	Don't. Smell will attract bears and takes too long	Store off-site on nearest non-earth planet	100/100 : Bears find highly appetizing
Fruits & Veggies	Devour passionately as if final meal	Consume raw. If flavor needed, use salt from tears	Store inside of metal barrel. Do not store berries. You are done with berries	40/100: Bears will only pursue if without meat for 2 hours
Dairy	Consume directly from cow udder	Shake in mouth while fleeing if you want butter or cheese	Store in sealed containers that can survive in space	90/100: Bears love ice cream and nachos
Alcohol	Chug	May garnish with olive or slice of lemon placed in left cheek	Store inside rotting carcass of dead sea lion	5-100/100* *Depends on alcohol. Bears prefer the hard stuff
Soy, Kale, other trash	Stomp on it then light it on fire	Pee on it	Flush down nearest toilet	0/100: However, if a bear catches you eating this it will kill you because you don't respect yourself
Honey	Lick directly off of bee legs	Prepare to be killed the moment you even try to eat honey	Store in honey bear container if you really want to die	100/100

Other Items to Lock Up

Nearly everything you own can and will be sought out by bears to be used as weapons against you. While it may be temporarily helpful to store things in a secure container, even a container will eventually be used against you. It is best to own nothing and to live nowhere. As long as bears are out there you should constantly be on the move with no attachments, material or human. Below are just a few examples of things you should not leave lying around.

Folding Chairs
If a bear gets ahold of your folding chairs, prepare for you, your family, your pets, and all surrounding wildlife to be chair-slammed.

Car Keys
Never let a bear come into possession of your car keys. *Bears are incredibly aggressive drivers.*

Toothbrush
Natural pranksters, bears will brush their anus with your toothbrush then return it to your toiletries.

Hot Dogs / SPAM / Balogna / Condensed Meat
Bears have the ability to resurrect condensed meat products and create things like hot-dog murder armies and bologna death hordes.

Ladders

Bears love using ladders to perform aerial attacks.

Assault Weapons

If a bear finds assault weapons, they are likely to sell them to international terrorists.

Chainsaws

If a bear gets ahold of a chainsaw, mass deforestation will soon follow.

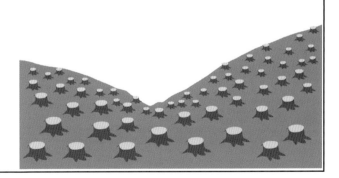

Explosives

Bears love surfing on explosions of all kinds.

PROPER BEAR AVOIDANCE

Hoping to go camping this year? Before you start planning, consider the danger of bear attacks. Here are five destinations that have proven to be the least dangerous when it comes to bear activity.

The Moon

It's rocky and devoid of life on the moon. Bears only like to kill where there is life.

The Moon is one of the nearest and most accessible destinations for families seeking safety from immediate bear attacks. Its low gravitational pull and lack of oxygen work wonders in deterring the predatory beasts. There were only a few dozen bear attacks recorded on the Moon in 2017, making it one of the most popular bear-safe destinations in the universe.

In the Earth's Core

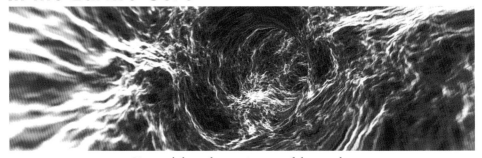

You can't beat the consistency of the weather.

The Earth's Core is perfect for dissuading ursine visitors, and who doesn't want to live where there is no chance of rain and the temperature remains warm even at night? Don't forget the marshmallows!

Atlantis

As long as salmon are not present you should be OK for a little while

Is Atlantis real? We don't know, but if you can find it, we are pretty sure bears haven't found it yet and it would be one of the most beautiful destinations on our list. Don't forget to pack the scuba gear!

On an Asteroid Careening Through Space

Make sure your tent is wind resistant.

Just like those guys in the movie Armageddon, you can camp out on a careening asteroid and suffer almost no bear attacks. The high winds make it hard to start a fire so be sure to bring a good camp stove.

Inside a Cow's Third Stomach

A cow's third stomach, also known as the omasum, is generally left alone by bears. Its elastic lining can fit almost anything with enough effort. If you can make it through the rumen and reticulum, you'll find safe harbor in the omasum. Just make sure you don't set up your new living space in the abomasum, a bear hot spot.

It's a tight squeeze, but then so is a coffin.

RadioShack

No one goes to RadioShack anymore. Not even bears.

Most people do not know what a radio or a shack is.

CHOOSING THE RIGHT FRIENDS

In a bear attack, the people you choose to associate with can have a huge impact on your survival. Bears attack based on a hierarchy of factors. For instance, they will often go after the most obese member of the group first. It is always a good idea to have at least one friend who is much fatter than you are. Make sure you are not too close with this person because when the time comes, you don't want your emotional attachment to get in the way of your survival. All emotional attachments should be abandoned if you hope to survive a bear attack.

Got a best friend? You may want to reconsider. Best friends are emotional attachments that can impede your split-second decision making in a bear attack. It's best to have no emotional attachments of any kind.

Did You Know?

You should never offer your child to a bear *without first covering it in honey.* Bears usually will pass up children or smaller people to favor larger adults. If a bear attacks you and all you have to put between it and yourself is a child, cover it with honey first to raise the chances the bear will choose it first.

Friend Selection Guidelines

	Friend Type	Advantages	Variables	Likeliness Bear Goes For Them Instead of You
	Athletic Friend	None. Avoid athletic friends as they have a better chance of leaving you to be killed.	If you are incredibly scrawny there is a small chance a bear will bypass you for the athletic friend.	Low. If an athlete has befriended you, chances are they are using you as protection.
	Fat Friend	Bears prefer high fat content and often go after the slowest moving target.	Though not all fat people are slow, bears still prefer the flavor of human lard.	Very high. Having an obese friend is imperative to preparing for a bear attack.
	Disabled Friend	Bears often go after the slowest among you, plus they are already pretty miserable anyway.	Bears may avoid someone wearing a full body cast to avoid eating too much gauze.	Highly likely, especially with leg injuries.
	Elderly Friend	If slow, the bear may target them if the bear is particularly lazy.	Bears do not favor the flavor or lack of muscle tissue in elderly people.	Only somewhat likely.
	Child	It is easy to lie to a child and tell them the bear is simply a man in a costume who wants to give them ice cream.	Unless a child is especially chubby or covered in salmon or honey, a bear will usually favor adult meat.	Only somewhat likely.
	Millennial	Tell a millennial it is racist to run from bears and they will immediately run toward the bear without question.	If a millennial has ingested too much laundry detergent bears will find them unappetizing.	Likely.
	Emotionally Needy Friend	Everyone has one they need to get rid of.	Make sure the emotional friend is distracted enough not to outrun you in a bear attack.	Likely.

HOLIDAY SURVIVAL

Many of the holidays we celebrate offer bears unique opportunities for attack. Humans often leave themselves more open on holidays as if bears also take the day off. Some say there is nothing we can do. Bears have declared war on Christmas, Thanksgiving, even Arbor Day. They have every intention of destroying every time-honored tradition we hold dear. But there are a few steps you can take that experts agree will decrease your chances of a bear attack by a good 7% if you are extremely lucky.

Avoid Salmon-Themed Decorations

Get rid of them.

Sure they are red and green which is really adorable when it comes to rustic, outdoorsy Christmas decorations. But any depiction of salmon, real or imagined, is an invitation for bear home invasion. Even paper or plastic decorations depicting salmon will attract bears. Avoid the topic altogether and focus on what's important: family.

Take Down the FREE HONEY Signs

Might as well write "Our Holiday Wish is Death."

It may be another time-honored tradition, but the "Free Honey" signs have got to go. In fact, even the signs that say "Honey: $1,000,000" need to go.

Let there be no hint of honey. If anything, hang signs that say, "Honey is Disgusting. God Hates Bees." Bears need to assume that there isn't a drop of honey anywhere near your domicile.

Remove All Teddy Bears from the Premises

No amount of tears is worth living in more danger of bears.

Ignore the weeping of your children. Their safety is more important than their joy. Teddy bears are a bear invention that not only desensitize your children to bear danger (more on that in the section on bear propaganda) but they contain tracking units that give bears your child's precise location.

Do Not Cook or Eat Anything

No amount of starvation is as bad as dying.

Pretty much any food will attract bears, so clear it all out at least one week before Christmas and don't bring anything back into the house until late January.

Lock All of Your Children in Bear Lockers

Kids are very resilient and can adjust to anything.

You will need to lock your children in bear lockers for their own safety. Some kids won't take kindly to such confinement but thanks to not eating for a week, most children will be fairly calm and compliant. They will need to remain in the lockers throughout Christmas Eve and all of Christmas Day. No presents should be opened, as the rustling can attract bears.

Only Invite Friends and Family You Despise

While we all have undesirable aunts who won't stop rubbing up against us, they should always be present in case of bear attacks.

The only thing worse than losing someone you love is knowing you could have gotten rid of someone you can't stand. You have an opportunity to thin the family out and remove some of the members who nobody liked in the first place. They all taste the same to a bear. If you know a bear will be showing up at your holiday meal, plan your seating arrangement accordingly. That guy your aunt married who clearly does drugs and will most likely divorce her some time after she spends thousands of dollars supporting his infantile choices? Sit him across from the bear. That hair-gel covered date rapist your daughter never should have married in the first place? Same with him. The 12-year-old nephew who does nothing but fling mashed potatoes and whine about his food and is destined to become the guy your daughter shouldn't have married? Sit him to the bear's right. Uncle Willy, the one who, no matter what you say, rolls his eyes and says "you're drinkin' the Kool aid!" then forces you to watch hours of conspiracy videos on YouTube? Sit him to the bear's left. With any luck, your next holiday meal could be a lot more pleasant if you play your cards right.

Christmas Tips

There's nothing more stressful than trying to enjoy Christmas with your family while bears are circling your home.

Kill Santa: Because bears are masters of disguise, anyone who tries to enter your house dressed as Santa should be killed immediately. There is no time to discern if the intruder is, or is not the real Santa. (Also applies to the Easter Bunny, the Tooth Fairy, etc.)

Make Sure Carolers Are Not Actually Bears: If there is a knock at your door, or the doorbell rings, make sure that the people on your porch are carolers and not bears. There are a few ways to be sure. You can tell them the neighbors just spilled a bunch of honey on accident. If the carolers drop everything and run to your neighbors' house, they are bears. They also can't sing complex carols. If they choose to sing something like "deck the halls" and mostly sing the "falalala" part, request that they sing something a little more complex like "Good King Wenceslas". If they mess it up, you know you've got bears.

Hire a Christmas Sniper: Because there is a good chance multiple bears could invade your front or back yard at once, it is smart to hire at least one Christmas Sniper. Try to find someone who has at least 100 confirmed kills. Trained snipers don't work for cheap, especially over holidays, so we suggest trying to get in on a Groupon if any become available.

What if a bear shows up for Thanksgiving?

While it is best to keep bears out, that isn't always possible. The following tips are for if a bear shows up to your Thanksgiving meal unexpectedly.

Thanksgiving can be hard if a combative bear shows up, but it doesn't have to be.

Don't pray too long. Bears are not only godless creatures, they are incredibly impatient. To set a roasted turkey, mashed potatoes, stuffing, gravy, yams and other dishes in front of a bear and then force it to sit still with its eyes closed while grandpa Otis rattles on about this great country, the pilgrims, Jesus's death on the cross, his sister Shirley's hip surgery, uncle Carl's gambling problem, football, and Duck Dynasty, all with annotated Bible quotes and long silent pauses, is a recipe for a heated bear attack. The prayer should be no longer than two or three words with minimal syllables.

Avoid eye contact. If you can help it, don't sit directly across the table from the bear. This is the worst place to sit because bears react aggressively to eye contact. They simply don't like being stared at, especially while they are trying to eat. Chances are, when the bear finally gets upset and starts attacking everyone, you will be the first to die. If you want to retain any hope of survival, do not sit across from the bear and do not stare at it.

Resist talking politics. It's very risky to talk politics around bears because they know the absolute correct position on any political issue and will rip your head off if you say anything that's wrong. But if you're really, really sure you're right about everything, go ahead.

Avoid alcohol. You need to be alert and ready. You can't allow for one misstep. One slip could cost you your life. This leads to our next point…

Accept that some family members will not make it out of this alive. This is the harsh truth of having a bear at Thanksgiving. It's not a question of will the bear attack everyone and kill them at random. It's a question of when. Will it be before or after pumpkin pie? Will the bear take a turkey nap then viciously attack or tear into the guests right after grandpa says grace? Whenever it is, you need to be ready. The bear is not here to enjoy a meal with you.

If you have time to plan ahead, put a bomb in the turkey. Not everyone has the luxury of preparing for a bear dropping in on Thanksgiving. Sometimes you'll get a warning, but often the beast will just show up and take a seat. If you have any lead time at all, you can really increase your chances of survival if you can fit your turkey with a bomb. The best way to distract a bear is to feed it delicious food that is secretly a bomb. Make sure the other family members are aware that they should not eat the turkey. When the bear goes for the bird, have a code word or phrase ready to alert the family to take cover. A word my family has used many times in the past is "Mayflower!" Upon shouting this code word, everyone should run as far as possible and hide behind something solid. With any luck, the bomb will go off inside the bear, momentarily confusing it and giving a few of you time to escape.

Halloween Tips

Halloween is an exciting time of year for children and parents alike, but bears love it too. To help ensure you have a safe and spooky holiday, here are some safety tips.

This should be obvious, but don't dress as a salmon or a jar of honey. Are you catching onto the theme? No salmon, no honey You'd be amazed how many people decide to dress as a large, shimmering sockeye salmon for Halloween. "Sexy Honey" is a popular costume as well. Both are a horrible idea if you are trying to avoid bear attacks. You're basically asking to get attacked. Instead, dress as something bears show little to no interest in, like cabbage, a business card, masking tape or a moth.

Bears love to trick-or-treat for trick-or-treaters.

Look both ways for bears before crossing the street. Another no-brainer but sadly many people don't look both ways for bears before crossing the street. Bears move at extreme speeds and they can always see you, even in a dark costume. Bears have heat sensor vision and can spot anything with blood circulating through their bodies. Always to your right and then your left. If you spot a bear in the distance, try to grab onto a passing vehicle and hold on. You will never outrun a bear on foot.

Don't trick-or-treat near streams where salmon are spawning. Make sure you aren't trick-or-treating in an area laden with hungry bears. Trick-or-treating near streams full of salmon or beehives full of sweet, dripping honey may be a tempting place to go knocking doors, but you'll be knocking on heaven's door if you keep that up because you're sure to run into a bear along the way.

Check your area with a bear locator app. A bear locator app such as GrizzAware™ or BearOverThere™ will use public records to let you know which houses in your area have recently been moved into by bears and offer you statistics such as kind of bear, height, weight, and known kills.

GrizzAware can be very helpful in locating registered bears in the area.

If a bear gives you candy, dispose of it immediately. No bear gives out candy just to be nice. Kindness is nowhere in the nature of a bear. Ursine logic is rooted in contempt for humanity and can never be trusted. If a bear gives you candy, throw it out, preferably into a volcano or vat of molten metal. Whether it's full of poison, razor blades or intestine melting acid, it's not going to be the sweet treat you hoped for.

Trick or Treat with someone large and slow. If a bear chases your group, the largest, slowest person will be eaten first. Try to get a neighbor to join you who doesn't get much exercise. Chances are you'd rather a bear eat them than your own family. Choose wisely, as bears tend to go for the largest member of the group because of their innate sense of greed.

If you dress as a bear and bears accept you into their sleuth, you can never leave. This is why dressing as a bear might not be a good idea. If they sniff you out and realize you are a fraud, you will be mauled to death. But if they are fooled by your costume, they may accept you as one of their own, in which case you will be forced to live the rest of your days as a bear because the moment you try to get away your cover will be blown.

Remember to have fun. Most importantly, take a deep breath and savor the moment. Give yourself permission to forget about the fact that bears are still 83% likely to devour you, and enjoy the holidays.

HOW TO BE READY FOR A BEAR ATTACK

Knowing that bears are coming for you, it would be irresponsible not to get your affairs in order before bears arrive. Here are some documents you should have prepared before bears arrive:

Bear Attack Preparation Checklist

☐ **Special Bequest of Personal Items:** List specific possessions you want to leave to designated people or organizations upon your death. *Don't stress!* These people will be killed by bears soon as well.

☐ **Funeral, Burial, Memorial Service:** Keep it simple. remember your loved ones will be trying not to be killed by bears while they try to make these

Getting your affairs in order before a bear kills you is the most considerate thing you can do for your family.

arrangements. We recommend burning the corpse and throwing it off an ocean cliff. DO NOT BURY REMAINS NEAR LIVING SPACE AS THE SMELL OF DEATH WILL ATTRACT MORE BEARS.

☐ **Important Personal Information:** Social security number, safety deposit box information, location of important papers, the name of your accountant, e-mail, cell Phone and other passwords, loans and mortgages, credit cards accounts, bank accounts, investments, non-liquid assets, insurance policies, unused Amazon gift cards, which books are hollowed out and have a gun inside, name on the tombstone where you buried the gold, etc.

☐ **List of People and Organizations to be Notified of Your Death:** Make sure to have the Bear Evisceration and Attack Record Organization (BEARO) notified if you break any records such as number of stabs or kicks in the testicles before death. When it comes to bear attacks, your legacy is all you have.

☐ **Intentions Upon Bear Attack:** It is good to put in writing how you intend to fight back when a bear attacks you because this is not always obvious to those observing or examining your remains (if any). Putting something in writing saying something like "my intention is to punch the bear repeatedly in the face as many times as possible before I die" will help the living weigh your intentions vs. what you actually did and decide if your death should be remembered with pride or derision.

☐ **Ownership of Pet(s) Upon Death:** Make certain that your pet(s) have a good home when you are slain by designating in writing who will be undertaking their care upon your death. Be sure to include important information about your pet. If you are willing to donate your dog to be strapped with explosives and sent into a crowd of bears please specify.

☐**Temporary Child Care Instructions:** Make sure the person you leave your children with is not some idiot who is just going to get killed by bears but has at least a fighting chance of lasting a few days longer than you.

☐ **Home Care Information:** List individuals and companies you have service contracts with and be sure to list any bear traps or land mines you have placed on your property.

☐ **Will:** Don't put too much time or money into this since bears will be killing everyone soon anyway.

Remember: These are just suggestions. Don't stress about these decisions as they are only important as long as other humans remain alive after you have passed on, which won't be long in the scheme of things.

Chapter 6
Bear Stealth Techniques

THE PERVASION OF BEARS into modern culture is far deeper than most people realize. Bears are masters of disguise, shape-shifters, time travelers, even ninjas. The common depiction of a bear as a furry land mammal who hibernates, eats honey, appears cuddly, and only occasionally attacks hikers is exactly the public image bears want us to see. What bears are truly up to and have been up to throughout history is their deepest, darkest secret.

COMMON BEAR DISGUISES

Bears have used disguises and other forms of trickery for centuries, permeating our culture and making us weak. They do this to distract us, soften us, and lower our guards. Much as the Russians meddled in the American election of 2016 to create seeds of discord within a harmoniously unified country, bears work in similar, but much more devious and far-reaching ways.

Check out the historical photos below. Look closely and you just might notice what you are looking at is actually an ursine imposter.

(LEFT) President Teddy Roosevelt next to a large globe. **(ABOVE)** World War 1 Pilot.

(ABOVE) Civil War soldier/banjo player. Most banjo players are bears in disguise. **(RIGHT)** Russian politicians. The one on the right is actually a bear.

(ABOVE) Compare the enhanced photo with the original. Can you spot the bear in this picture? **(BELOW CENTER)** Many football players are bears in disguise, using brain injuries to weaken the human gene pool. **(BOTTOM)** Bears disguise themselves as pilots, flying airliners without proper licensing, putting us all in danger.

(ABOVE LEFT) A bear sells ice cream, coaxing neighborhood children who should be eating kale. **(ABOVE RIGHT)** Bears run rampant in the legal system, working as judges, attorneys, and even stacking juries.

(ABOVE LEFT) Bears seek out trusted positions, such as grade school teachers. **(BOTTOM LEFT)** Bears have been working in Hollywood since the dawn of film. **(ABOVE RIGHT)** Bears even disguise themselves as common workers.

PLACES BEARS MIGHT BE HIDING RIGHT NOW

Most people know to watch out for bears when they are at Yosemite National Park, anywhere in Alaska, or in an elementary school in Wyoming. But most people don't realize how many other places these deadly creatures can be found. What follows is a list of some of the most common places bears hide.

Couch Cushions

It's a common place to lose keys, remote controls, even celery. The cushions of a couch are a great place to hide, and bears know this. Next time you go to sit down, think again. <u>Never</u> sit on a couch.

Bears are naturally cushioned and soft, making the couch an ideal place to blend in and wait for victims.

Artificial Sweeteners

By offering the taste of sweetness without any calories, artificial sweeteners seem like a dream come true. The average 12-ounce can of sugar-sweetened soda delivers about 150 calories, almost all of them from sugar. The same amount of diet soda—zero calories. The choice seems like a no-brainer, but what companies like Splenda, Sweet'N Low, and Equal don't want you to know is that their sweeteners come with a much higher risk of bear attack.

Depending on which studies you look at, bear attack risk in the vicinity of artificial sweeteners is heightened by anywhere from 14% to 27%. Is the risk worth it? I guess that depends on how much you love soda.

How do artificial sweeteners help you lose weight? By bears killing you.

Dense Body Hair

Though it is often seen as a sign of masculinity, dense body hair can be a popular nesting place for violent bears. It is recommended that the hirsute keep body hair trimmed or even fully removed to avoid attacks. If you discover a bear in your body hair, it's too late to get waxed.

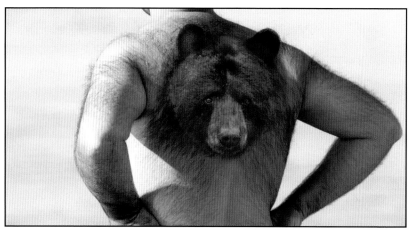

Thick back hair may attract the opposite sex, or even the same sex. But it also attracts bears.

In the Spare Tire Compartment of a '93 Dodge Neon

The Dodge Neon was a popular car in the '90s, but starting in the early 2000s, bear attacks on owners of the cars became rampant. Bears had been hiding in the spare tire compartment and springing out at unsuspecting victims who were unloading their trunks. A factory recall was issued, costing Dodge nearly $6,000,000,000 in lawsuits. If you or anyone you know owns this car, it is advised that you take it in immediately to have the issue fixed.

You can buy a Dodge, but you can't dodge a bear attack.

Gender-Neutral Restrooms

Some people feel that gender-neutral restrooms pose unforeseen risks on society. They are correct. Bears frequently wait in the stalls of these bathrooms and attack without provocation.

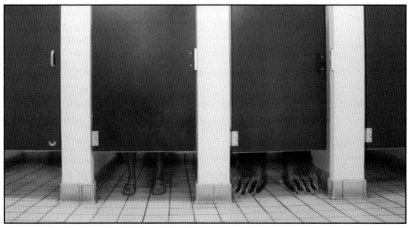

If the guy in the stall next to you grunts more than ex-pected, it's probably a bear.

BEAR SCAMS AND PROPAGANDA

Bear propaganda has invaded many cultures. From fabric softener to honey bottles to toilet paper commercials, bears are portrayed as cuddly, soft, and fun to snuggle with. Bear journalist Jonah Goldberg has pointed out that Coca-Cola runs Christmastime commercials featuring polar-bear families celebrating the season. But polar bears don't live in intact nuclear families. The males are deadbeat dads who eat their own children sometimes. This is the last thing anyone should do on Christmas. Coca-Cola is only one small example of bear propaganda in pop culture leading mankind down a dangerous path.

Below are some of the most popular ways bears use propaganda to coax us into a naive complacency and make us more vulnerable to bear attacks.

Teddy Bears

If it isn't obvious how devious bear propaganda can be, Exhibit A is their targeting of youth. Teddy bear culture perpetuates the lie that bears just want a hug. The plush toys fill our children's rooms, cartoons, commercials, and toy stores. Children are pummeled with teddy bear propaganda from the day they are born.

Children with teddy bears are highly likely to walk straight into a bear attack.

Gummy Bears

Gummy bears are an alien species of bear in a cryo-sleep state. Much like a sea monkey, the gummy bear is a gelatinous creature in a state of temporary stasis. They become reactivated by human digestive fluids, often devouring us slowly from the inside. Even worse, they contain corn syrup.

A real gummy bear is a mutated glob of horrible, acidic goo that suffocates you and melts your face off of your skull. That's not delicious.

Sports Teams

Bears are popular mascots because they embody fearlessness and ferocity. But bears have infiltrated many of the most successful teams as coaches and players, fooling sports fans into cheering and even calling for the slaughter of other teams by bears.

There's nothing as intense as being chewed out on the bench by an angry grizzly bear.

Bears in Gay Culture

The gay community has already suffered many attacks, but none are worse than bears using gay "bear" culture to coax men seeking husky, hirsute partners into a deadly bear attack.

Men who seek to hook up with bears often get hooked up with actual bears.

Bear Claws

This tasty pastry was designed to encourage people to walk around longing to get a bear claw right in the face. Many people who order bear claws get more than they bargained for.

Putting a bear claw in your face increases your chances of getting a real bear claw to the face.

CELEBRITY BEARS IN POP CULTURE

Bears permeate media, but did you know that many of the cuddly bears you know from pop culture are based on some of the most violent bears in history? Well, it's true. Behind every silly cartoon bear is a tale of death, loss of life, and people not being alive anymore.

Smokey the Bear

The real "Smokey" was a pyromaniac grizzly bear from North Dakota. Wildlife authorities recorded stories of a grizzly in the mountains of North Dakota who became obsessed with setting fire to small villages after an accident involving a gas station, a bee hive, and a box of matches. The bear's first experience with fire may have been an accident, but after that, it became an addiction. The ursine maniac burned down campgrounds, forests, small towns, and lodges; always finding a fuel source and a way to light it; often using campfires that had not been fully extinguished, and discarded cigarette butts to ignite the blaze. Signs were posted with an image of the bear standing over the charred corpses of campers with the slogan, "Only you can prevent forest fires." Over time, marketing people got their hands on the image and tried to make it "less dark." Soon, the image was tamed until the Smokey we know today was born.

The real Smokey Bear loved taking selfies at his burn sites.

The Bear in the Big Blue House

The real Blue House Bear systematically obliterated blue houses. Nobody knows how one of the most horrific tales of ursine terror became an adorable kids' show. The original Bear in the Big Blue House was simply a murderous beast with an affinity for houses painted cool shades of blue. The beast often entered in the early morning, driving the family out or eating them in their beds. The creature would go on to devour everything in the fridge, pantry, fish tank, and garbage cans. Furniture would be torn to pieces, drywall caved in, water pipes busted, ceiling fans torn down, windows smashed, paint cans dumped, tiles torn up, and ice cube trays dumped and left out on the counter, not refilled.

The beast always managed to elude authorities until an expensive operation was put in place to defeat it. Law enforcement and wildlife service personnel constructed a blue house near the forest and filled it with delicious meats. When the bear inevitably entered, the house was blown up using

three hundred pounds of TNT. Disney bought the rights to the story and, after many script revisions, *Bear in the Big Blue House* was born.

No blue house was safe if this bear was in town.

Yogi Bear

The real Yogi didn't steal picnic baskets, he stole people's right to live.
The fun-loving, wisecracking bear of Hanna-Barbera fame has his origins in something much darker than basket thievery. The original Yogi lived in the Great Smoky Mountains and became obsessed with eating picnickers. The bear often struck with such quickness that authorities would arrive only to find a scattered scene of horror. At one point, the bear tore into a family so fast that the necktie of one of his victims became entangled on his neck and stayed there. The green tie became a flag of death for peaceful picnickers. Eventually, a decoy picnic was set up with lifelike cybernetic picnickers made of explosives. Yogi took the bait and was blown to smithereens, but his legacy was carried on in his famous cartoon counterpart.

One of the warning signs at Yellowstone Park when Yogi was at large.

Care Bears

The original care bear stare was all staring and no caring. Nobody knows how the original "Stare Bears" of Salmonhook, AK got their abilities. Stories were told of a *sleuth of mother bears who would form a line and stare down other wildlife. The victims, often moose, caribou, or elk, would freeze up as their eyes began to sizzle in their sockets. Soon their insides would liquefy and evacuate from the animal's orifices. The bears would proceed to devour the charred beasts. But one day the bears faced off with a group of hunters and their taste for human flesh became insatiable. At first, they were only going after hikers and campers, but eventually they made their way to the small mountain town of Antler Hill and took out every living

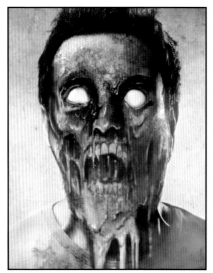

person, including police and military who had arrived to stop them. The decision was made by the government to nuke the city so that the entire place would be obliterated from existence. They did not want history to record such a horrible occurrence. Nobody knows if the "Stare Bears" were in the blast, but you will never find mention of Antler Hill in any history book. Some say they are still at large.

Actual victim of a Care Bear stare.

*A group of bears is called a sleuth

Winnie the Pooh

Winnie the Pooh was a honey-drunk brown bear who enslaved millions of beekeepers and crapped mountains of honey. The original Winnie the Pooh was anything but silly. The real bear was from the mountains of Russia. The local villagers called the creature "Medzver" (the Honey Beast) because it obsessively attacked honey plantations and devoured so much honey that it would have fits of sticky, liquid, golden diarrhea. Though the bear hungered only for honey and never human flesh, this beast still made plenty of human lives a living hell. Once the creature realized men could harvest honey, it single-handedly enslaved millions, forcing them to work on large honey plantations so the bear could be fed honey with a constantly running firehose. The bear died of diabetes atop a mountain of its own golden feces, earning it the nickname "Poo Bear".

This photo was taken at one of Pooh's beekeeper internment camps.

Gladly, the Cross-Eyed Bear

After a bear named Gladly escaped a local circus in Klitch, MO, it attacked a local bar and drank over thirty-two gallons of liquor. The drunken bear then attacked the nearby Flaming Bible Baptist Church, eating seventeen of the patrons (over half the congregation). In mourning, the church wrote a hymn about the incident, but over time the lyrics were misunderstood and replaced with the current iteration, "Gladly, the Cross I'd Bear."

When asked what Gladly the Cross-Eyed Bear was like, one church member said he was like Gary Busey with a taste for human flesh.

Other Bear Propaganda

Bear imagery has become ubiquitous across all forms of media. Myrtlewood carvings, t-shirts, salt and pepper shakers, beer logos, and more carry the animal's likeness, adding to the cloud of ignorance mankind exists within. To name them all would fill a million books, but the point is a simple one. Don't fall for it.

The above logo was obviously designed to lure surfers to the coast of California to be slain by bears.

BEARS AND ONLINE DATING

Have you ever read an online dating profile that sounded too good to be true? Tall, dark, rugged, loves fishing and the outdoors? Needs his time in the cave but loves spending time with his honey, too? One blurry photo of a riverbank as an avatar, a man of few words, mysterious, rugged, an outdoorsy type? Careful, you could end up on a date with a 1,600-pound Alaskan grizzly bear.

Since the invention of the Internet, the way we find love has changed dramatically. The way bears find people to murder has changed as well. Bears love apps like Tinder, Match, and other free dating services. (Bears don't use eHarmony. They can't endure the long list of questions and resent the cost of subscription.) To bears, these romance finding services are the Grub Hub of the bear world. To them, these companies provide a detailed menu with pictures and descriptions, and an option for delivery.

Because so few human men know how to write appealing profile descriptions, bears have a distinct advantage in that the basic qualities of a bear tend to be much more attractive to human females (strong, a provider, hairy, a protector) than the kinds of things human males often brag about on their dating profiles such as their preferred hair gel, their love of the band Iron and Wine, comic books, and raising Sea Monkeys.

If your date is a bear and asks to try your salmon, hand it over.

Five Clues Your Match Might Be a Bear

1. **Misleading photo:** Bears often take photos from flattering angles. Others use images of freshly caught salmon. Some go so far as to steal the profile pictures of human men after killing them.

2. **Doesn't ever want to meet at his place:** Bears often move to where the salmon are easiest to catch. They never have one permanent address and will always want to go to your place.

3. **Only wants to eat at a place with good salmon:** Want to meet at that cute new coffee shop in Silver Lake? Good luck. Bears can't stand to go anywhere salmon isn't served. It may sound like a fancy night out,

but chances are it'll be an ugly night of death.

4. **Constant misspellings in texts and emails:** Because of their long claws, bears have a hard time with touchscreens and keyboards. If your potential man sends you a lot of misspelled words, chances are he's no man at all.

5. **Uses the word "honey" too much:** Many women see the word 'honey' as a microaggression. Coming from bears, it's a macroaggression. Bears are obsessive when it comes to honey. If your potential partner is constantly referring to a desire for honey, there's a good chance you are chatting with a bruin.

Example of a bear's online dating profile.

Chapter 7
What to Do in a Bear Attack

THE MOMENT HAS COME. You have crossed paths with fate, and a 1,650-pound grizzly bear is staring at you. You might have been on a hike, or at the grocery store, or even on a plane. Nobody knows when a bear will cross their path. That is why it is so important to know your options before the time comes.

What To Do When a Bear Spots You

There are a lot of misconceptions about what to do when a bear sees you. People will put all kinds of pressure on you to "try to make yourself look bigger", or "if it's black, fight back, if it's brown, lie down", and the most common, "shoot it." Few people realize that if a bear sees you, *you're already dead*. It's just a matter of time. You should keep this in mind as you decide how to respond.

COMMON MISTAKES

In this section we will look at the many mistakes people make in bear confrontations, from our basic understanding of what is going on in a bear's head, to reactions that seem instinctual (such as wetting your pants), and shooting guns at them. Nearly every commonly suggested course of action in a confrontation with a bear is wrong.

You cannot purchase your life with fresh salmon.

Did You Know?

Bears use an enhanced viewing system, much like the visualizing software of a murderous cyborg from the future. When a bear surveys an area, it immediately assesses vulnerability, attack hierarchy, potential threats, environmental attack potential, and more.

▲ Unlike man-made cyborgs, bears have a completely organic cybernetic retinal system that is with them from the day they are born. With this system, bears can instantly look up a person's information and make an instantaneous attack assessment.

▲ The naturally occurring database in a bear's eye contains ten times the information of the human Internet.

Am I Experiencing a Bear Attack?

How does one know if they are in a bear attack? The beginning stages of a bear attack can easily be mistaken for other symptoms such as indigestion, gout, and rabies. It's good to know all the symptoms of a bear attack so that you know for sure if you are in a hopeless situation.

COMMON BEAR ATTACK SYMPTOMS

Sweating / Outbursts

Involuntary Urination

Diarrhea / Vomiting

Severe Headache

Dizziness

Sore Neck / Back Pain

Sudden Blackouts

Congested Breathing / Suicidal Thoughts

Ripped in Half

WHAT DO YOU DO WI

A bear's stare can be unnerving. Here are some common responses to being stared at by a bear.

Freeze

Try to Make Yourself Bigger

Climb Nearest Tree

Offer Your Child

Lay Down

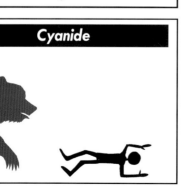

Cyanide

N A BEAR SPOTS YOU?

Please note: none of these responses are effective whatsoever in stopping a bear.

Jump Off Nearest Cliff

Kick Bear in Junk

PUNT
PUNT
PUNT

Blow Rape Whistle

Offer Large Salmon

Cover Self in Mud or Feces

Bear Spray

MIST

Stop, Think, Go Balls Out

If you have been spotted by a bear, it's important to put things into perspective. First, **STOP** and realize that the thing looking at you is a bear. You are not a bear. Acknowledge that it has control of the situation.

Next, **THINK** about your family, your friends, your wife, your girlfriend. Think about how people are going to remember you. In the digital age, you never know who might be filming. You need to think about how you want to remembered in this moment.

Finally, **GO BALLS OUT**. Die on your terms. Get a good punch or kick in there. Do something epic. Imagine the headline or the news report about your death. Make your loved ones proud. This moment will define you for ages to come.

To review:

STOP:
Acknowledge that you are already dead.

THINK:
Consider how you would like to be remembered.

BALLS OUT:
Just do the most badass insane thing you can come up with.

Be Remembered Well

If you do something awesome before a bear kills you, there is a good chance it will be the thing that is put on your tombstone. Everything about you will be forgotten except this one thing, so make it count. Nobody wants "Bear killed him and he just screamed" as an epitaph.

HERE LIES
WANDA SHERRATT
(AUGUST 18, 1959 – MAY 23, 2016)

KILLED BY A BEAR
BUT NOT BEFORE GIVING IT
A PURPLE NURPLE

HERE LIES
Chris Wynter
(March 13, 1989 – July 2, 2009)

Kneed a bear in the nuts
just before it killed him

We're proud of you, Chris

HERE LIES
DIANE BEGGS
(JANUARY 26, 1951 – JULY 2, 2009)

BELOVED DAUGHTER,
MOTHER,
GRANDMOTHER
AND BEAR PUNCHER.

"Though it slay me,
the bear I punch it"

Here Lies
Sean Whitley
(August 16, 1971 – Oct. 31, 2012)

Brother, son, but most of all,
the man who valiantly unleashed
a stream of diarrhea into
a bear's face.
He died a Hero

HOW TO TELL IF A BEAR IS STALKING YOU

Sometimes a bear doesn't kill you immediately. It first stalks you relentlessly. Being stalked by a bear is one of the most dreaded experiences anyone can face. Do you know all the signs you are being stalked by a bear? Read on for expert tips on how to tell if you have a grizzly on your tail and what you can do about it.

#1. It takes a second look

Remember, bears see you naked.

This is the first sign a passing bear might think about paying you another visit. They look, and then they look again. Watch those eyes. If they take that second look, they see something they want.

#2. Check for paw prints or fresh droppings nearby

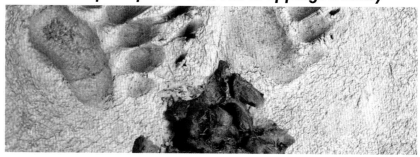

To test droppings to see if they belong to a bear, see if they taste like dead unicorns.

Think the bear didn't follow? Think again. Check any areas near your home where paw prints could be left. Check your lawn for droppings. If you find anything, lock your door. You have a stalker.

#3. Constant Gifts

Remember, a bear only gives because it wants something.

Honey on your car. Flowers in your mailbox. Salmon on your doorstep. A stalking bear will pretend like they're just being thoughtful, but in truth, you're all they can think about.

#4. You keep "running into" each other when you're out

If you see a bear anywhere besides near a salmon-filled stream, exercise great suspicion.

Suddenly everywhere you go, there's the bear. The library, the video rental store, the yarn shop, the courthouse, your cousin Amy's house. Places they never frequented before, now they are always there, acting like they just happen to be there at the same time as you. Don't let them fool you. If a bear keeps showing up when you are out and about, you're being stalked like celery.

#5. Constant phone calls

Be wary of calls coming in from Alaska.

The phone rings, you say hello, and all you hear is heavy panting and breathing. You are seriously regretting giving this bear your number. Now it's getting serious. Get caller ID and don't answer it when the bear calls, whatever you do. Answering only stokes the flames.

#6. It keeps "accidentally" leaving things at your house

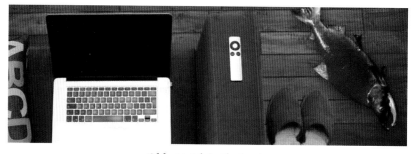

Oldest trick in the book.

Maybe your bear started out as a friend or has suddenly become buddies with your roommate. Whatever the case, if they can, they will continually "accidentally" leave things laying around just so they have a reason to pop in on you whenever they want. It's best to mail the items back, or drive out to the woods and throw them out the window. Don't play its games. That's exactly what the bear wants.

#7. Your dog is dead

Better get dog life insurance.

You go outside to mow your lawn and find your dog ripped apart. Not eaten, just ripped apart in a fit of jealous rage. Now things have reached a new level. We suggest you go stay with relatives out of state.

#8. It chases you down the interstate and tries to rip the doors off your car

Bears are fast on land, even faster on the freeway.

Bear chasing your car down the freeway, clawing at your tires? Trying to rip your car to pieces? Nine out of ten times you've got a stalker problem. Floor it. Who cares if the cops catch you. At least they have guns and might be able to protect you.

#9. It kills police and military to get to you

This is not healthy, friendly behavior.

If this has happened to you, it's time to face facts. You have a stalker bear. You need to go to the police station and file a police report, once they restaff. After you've done that, stock up on weapons of any kind. Look in your garage. Axes, fire, gasoline, chainsaws. Whatever you can to defend yourself, do it.

#10. It walks through flames with an axe in its skull and still tries to get to you

Bears are big believers in the power of perseverance.

Let me guess? You tried to douse this persistent bear with gasoline, set it on fire, and pound it in the head with an axe? Looks like the only fire you ignited was this bear's flaming obsession. It looks like somebody can't take no for an answer.

#11. It kills you

100% of bear stalkings end in death.

Most signs are up to interpretation, but this one's pretty cut and dried. If the bear killed you, it was stalking you. Unless it was a clear accident. Having a stalker is a miserable experience. Hopefully, by reading this book you can make more informed decisions from now on.

Did You Know?

Not all bear stalking stories have a sad ending. Every once in a while, the person being stalked will come around to the bear's advances and they will wind up getting married.

Of course, the first time there is an argument of any kind, the bear will then kill their victim. Bears are never willing to put in the required work to develop a solid and long-lasting relationship.

WHAT TO DO IF A BEAR CHASES YOU UP A TREE

Getting chased into a tree is not ideal. You don't want people to think you are a coward or some kind of idiot who thinks bears can't climb trees. Whatever the reason, tree climbing is a common occurrence in bear attacks. Often, the person in the tree fails to make the best of a bad situation. Let's explore some of the things you can do if a bear has chased you up a tree.

Bears love chasing people up trees to see what kind of things they will do before they climb up and eat them.

Option #1

THROW PINE CONES AT IT

This is one thing you could do instead of just sit there.

Option #2

TRY TO PEE IN THE BEAR'S EYE

This takes practice because bears have tiny eyes, but if you pull it off you can say you did something impressive before you died.

Option #3

THROW
SQUIRRELS AT IT

Another great way to pass the time
before you die.

Option #4

BEAT YOURSELF
WITH STICKS

It's normal to completely lose your mind
at this point.

Option #5

TELL IT YOUR LIFE STORY

It will enjoy killing you more.

Option #6

TRY TO ATOMIC ELBOW IT

Better to die a man's death.

Option #7

COVER YOURSELF IN FECES AND SET YOURSELF ON FIRE

"When in Rome."

Option #8

USE VENTRILOQUISM TO MAKE THE BEAR THINK THE TREE IS AN ENT

Bears don't read Tolkien, but it's fun.

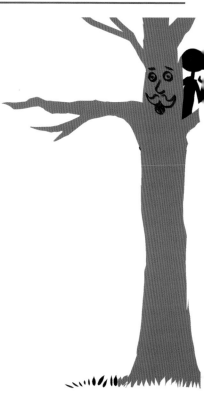

WHAT TO DO IF A BEAR PULLS UP NEXT TO YOU AT A RED LIGHT

Ever been at a red light and suddenly there's a bear one lane over giving you the staredown? Here are some no-nonsense steps to take if you ever find yourself in this situation.

1.) Pretend you don't notice it: Bears feed on attention. If you make eye contact, chances are they will take that as a cue to begin verbally harassing you. Don't play into it.

2.) Slowly roll up all windows: Try to do this casually. If a bear thinks you may be rolling up the windows to protect yourself, they may attack prematurely.

3.) Turn down your stereo, especially if you are listening to "The Bear Necessities": This should be obvious.

Bears are incredibly aggressive, especially behind the wheel.

4.) Do not rev your engine unless the bear does: Never provoke a bear, especially at a stoplight. But if the bear revs their engine, rev yours back. Not responding at this point would be seen as a sign of weakness.

#5.) When the light turns green, punch the gas hard: Bears are vicious, but they have slow reaction time. Try to be prepared for the light to turn green and to get off the line first. This is crucial to any chance you may have of survival.

#6.) Try to crash into a salmon truck or honey farm: Your only chance of escape is to crash somewhere that will redirect the bear's attention. A salmon or honey farm is a great option (though you should always remember to be careful of bees when crashing into a honey farm). If you can't find a suitable crash site, try to drive off of a cliff or hillside that is high enough to guarantee an unsurvivable fall. You do not want to crash and to live long enough to experience what the bear will inevitably do to you.

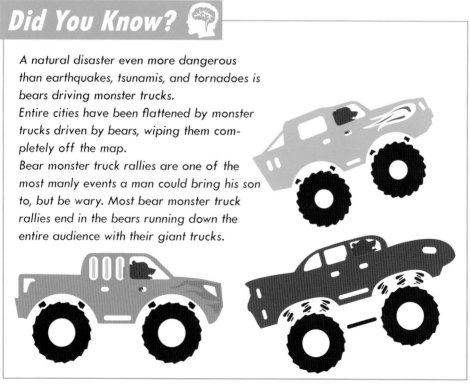

Did You Know?

A natural disaster even more dangerous than earthquakes, tsunamis, and tornadoes is bears driving monster trucks.

Entire cities have been flattened by monster trucks driven by bears, wiping them completely off the map.

Bear monster truck rallies are one of the most manly events a man could bring his son to, but be wary. Most bear monster truck rallies end in the bears running down the entire audience with their giant trucks.

BASIC CAR SAFETY

Even if you don't find yourself at a stop light next to a bear, you still must consciously practice proper vehicular bear safety at all times.

X DON'T *LEAVE FOOD IN A PARKED CAR*

BEARS WILL EAT YOUR FOOD

After removing food from your car, hose it out with boiling water to get rid of the residual odor, which could still attract bears.

X DON'T *LEAVE A DOG IN A PARKED CAR*

BEARS THROW DOGS VERY FAR

Bears can often be seen skipping dogs across the surface of ponds, much like humans do with pebbles.

✗ DON'T *LEAVE GRANDMA IN A PARKED CAR*

BEARS PUSH OLD LADIES TO THE TOP OF MOUNTAINS JUST TO WATCH THEM ROLL DOWN SUPER FAST

This is why you should always make sure Grandma is buckled in.

✗ DON'T *PARK A CAR UNDER A TREE*

BEARS ELBOW-DROP PARKED CARS

This is one reason it is good to wear a helmet while driving.

✗ DON'T *PARK IN A ROW OF OTHER CARS*

WHY?

BEARS WILL RUN OVER THEM IN MONSTER TRUCKS

No bear can resist a bunch of cars lined up and ready to be smashed.

✗ DON'T *TRY TO RUN OVER A BEAR*

WHY?

BEARS WILL PILEDRIVE YOUR ENTIRE CAR

There is nothing a bear cannot piledrive.

WHAT TO DO IF A BEAR IS CHASING YOU AND YOU ARE ON FIRE

Life can put you into all sorts of crazy situations. Ever been chased by a bear while on fire? Most of us don't ever think we'd end up being that guy. It's good to have a plan for all situations, and you should always be prepared with a plan just in case you ever find yourself in this situation.

STOP

DROP

ROLL

COVER YOURSELF IN HONEY

The bear will kill you faster if you taste like honey barbecue.

Chapter 8
A Guide to Bear Fighting

LIFE IS A SERIES OF BATTLES. We battle our own insecurities, our bad habits, our shortcomings, and our circumstances. But one of the greatest battles of your life will be the moment a bear attacks you. Of all life's figurative and literal fights, this will be your most harrowing.

Bear fighting is not for everyone. It requires a willingness to throw all caution to the wind, and to face your enemy knowing that the chances of you winning are 0% and yet holding onto hope that somehow it will still all be worth it. Kicking and punching a bear can often anger it and cause it to kill you in a much more violent way. Bear fighting is high-risk. It is not for the weak.

If you have decided that you want to go out swinging, this chapter will outline some of the attacks you can attempt in that final confrontation.

GETTING WARMED UP

Before you go looking for a bear fight, you should get warmed up. Besides some light stretching, here are some exercises to prepare you for your confrontation.

BEAR FIGHTING WARM-UPS

Backwards Crab Crawls
There is a good chance you will be crab crawling away from a bear once it knocks you down. Make sure to scream a lot and shout NO! NO!

Organ Gathering Practice
Before you are gathering your innards and trying to carry them and run, practice using potatoes or an armload of canned peaches.

Chest Press at least 1,600 lbs.
If this is more than you can lift, perfect. That's exactly what it will feel like when the bear is on top of you.

Friend Tossing
If you need to throw someone at the bear, make sure you get some practice. People are hard to throw.

Car Door Head Slams
To simulate having your head bitten by a bear, try slamming your head repeatedly in a car door. If you find this difficult, find a friend or family member to help. You'd be surprised how much people enjoy being a part of this warm-up.

Walk Onto a Busy Freeway
Much like boxers spar using softer impact hits and heavier protective gear, a good way to simulate a sparring-level version of the beating you will undergo with a bear is by stepping onto a busy freeway and being run over repeatedly.

Bear Fighting Techniques

Below are just some of the moves you can attempt against a bear, and their effectiveness ratings.

Punch to the Gut

X INEFFECTIVE

Punch to the Face

X INEFFECTIVE

Jumping Face Kick

X INEFFECTIVE

Spinning Roundhouse Kick

X INEFFECTIVE

Bear Fighting Techniques (Cont.)

Knee to the Face

X INEFFECTIVE

Upside-Down Breakdancer Kick

X INEFFECTIVE

Double Knee Drop

X INEFFECTIVE

Elbow Drop

X INEFFECTIVE

Suplex

X INEFFECTIVE

Piledriver

X INEFFECTIVE

Sedan Ram

X INEFFECTIVE

Using Jiu Jitsu to Fight a Bear

The amazing thing about Jiu Jitsu is that it doesn't matter what your size is. Little guys can use it to take on big guys, and people of any size can use it against a bear and get similar results.

1. WAIT
Let the bear make the first move.

2. DUCK AND SHOOT
When the bear attacks, duck and shoot in.

3. TAKE THE BACK
Work your way around and take the bear's back.

4. NOTE:

It won't be able to reach because of its short arms.

5. CHOKE

Go for a rear naked choke.

6. WAIT

Eventually the bear will pass out and fall forward. You did it!

7. WAKE UP

Now snap out of your fantasy and realize you died somewhere around step 2.

Using Jiu Jitsu to Anticipate Bear Attacks

One of the key principles of Jiu Jitsu is knowing your opponent's attacks before they execute them. If you know every option your opponent has at any point in the fight, you can anticipate and counter that attack with something more effective.

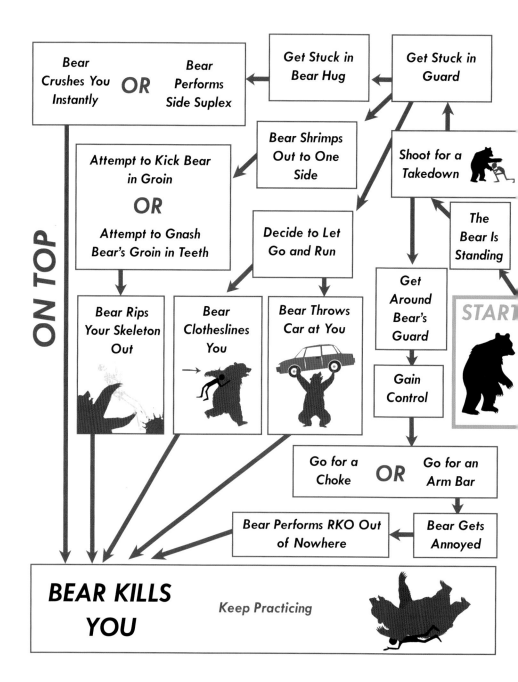

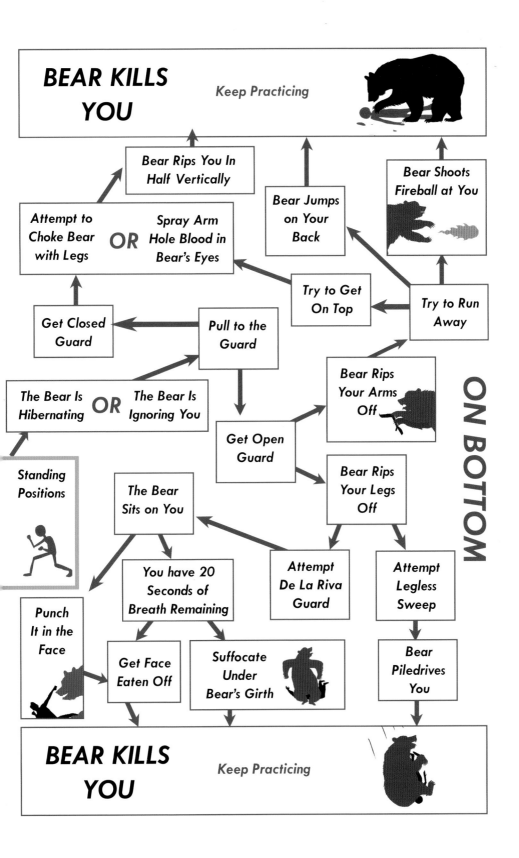

VARIOUS ESCAPES

If a bear is coming at you or has you in a hold, it is important to know the proper escape. With the right strategy, you could increase your lifespan by seconds.

Headlock Escape

If a bear has you in a headlock, try this simple maneuver to get out of it.

1. Just before bear comes in for headlock, remove head.

2. Discard

*PLEASE TRY TO DISCARD YOUR HEAD IN A PROPER HEAD RECYCLING CONTAINER IF AT ALL POSSIBLE. YOU DON'T WANT TO DIE A LITTERBUG.

Arm Bar Escape

At first, escaping an arm bar seems impossible, especially with a bear. But if you act quickly and methodically, you don't have to succumb to this brutal submission hold.

1. The bear is going for an arm bar. What can you do?

2. Quickly clasp your hands together to buy some time.

3. Turn left and feed elbow through.

4. Lift head and shrimp toward your feet.

5. Chew the hell out of your arm until it detaches. *KEEP LEFT LEG DOWN.*

6. You've escaped! Now go have a nervous breakdown and bleed out until the bear finds you.

173.

How to Escape From a Bear Every Time

You may be getting the sense that escaping from a bear is nearly impossible. That is true. But the good news is there is always a way to escape a bear, and despite the fact that you can never defeat a bear, you can almost always escape from one.

1. WAIT
Let the bear come to you.

2. LET IT HAPPEN
Lie down and let the bear eat your entire body.

3. ESCAPE
After the bear digests you, you will escape right out of its butt.

GOOD JOB

PROPER BEAR PUNCHING

If you've decided to punch a bear, make sure you do it properly. Punching a bear correctly will have a major effect on how things pan out.

WRONG!

Never punch a bear directly in the face!

The bear's hard skull will break your hand, then you will be killed.

RIGHT

Punch the bear directly in the nose. *(This is the softest part of its head.)*

This way you won't suffer a broken hand while being mauled.

PREDICTING THE BEAR'S NEXT MOVE

It's important to know what will happen next in a bear fight so that the bear doesn't have the element of surprise. In this section, we will look at typical actions a bear might take and what you can expect. By anticipating the bear's move, you can avoid having a stupid look of surprise when the bear kills you.

Situation: **BEAR APPROACHES FROM BEHIND**

WHAT TO EXPECT

SUPLEX

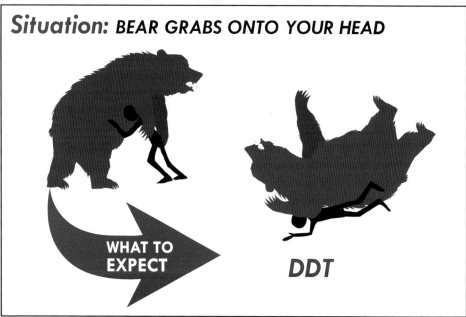

Situation: **BEAR GRABS ONTO YOUR HEAD**

WHAT TO EXPECT

DDT

Predicting a Bear's Next Move

Situation: BEAR THROWS YOU INTO THE VINES

WHAT TO EXPECT

CLOTHESLINE

Situation: BEAR WRAPS YOUR ARMS UP

WHAT TO EXPECT

DOUBLE UNDERHOOK POWERBOMB

Situation: *BEAR RAISES YOU OVER HEAD*

WHAT TO EXPECT

GORILLA PRESS SLAM

Situation: *BEAR PLACES YOUR FEET ON BRANCH*

WHAT TO EXPECT

DRAGON SCREW NECK WHIP

Situation: BEAR GOES FOR A CHAIR

WHAT TO EXPECT

CHAIR SLAM

Situation: BEAR CARRIES YOU UP STEEP HILL

WHAT TO EXPECT

PILEDRIVER

Predicting a Bear's Next Move (Cont.)

Situation: *BEAR GOES INTO A CROUCH*

WHAT TO EXPECT

UPPERCUT INTO THE SUN

Situation: *BEAR LOGS ONTO COMPUTER*

WHAT TO EXPECT

EPIC TROLLING

IF A BEAR ATTACKS YOU AND ALL YOU HAVE IS A KNIFE

A knife is not the ideal weapon in a bear fight, but it can be useful.

1. Remain calm, be still. Let the bear come to you.

2. Stab repeatedly until you die.

You are going to die anyway. Might as well try to beat the record for most pre-death bear stabs, which is 12.

WHAT NOT TO DO

Unfortunately, most people who engage in a fight with a bear make a lot of mistakes. Like many high-pressure situations, fighting a bear can be highly stressful, and it is well documented that people make bad decisions when they are under immense stress. Here are some of the most popular mistakes people make when trying to fight a bear.

Mistake #1:

Trying to Cover Your Face and Genitals

While your instincts may be to cover up your most sensitive areas, attempting to shield yourself with your hands is futile. If a bear wants to go for your face or genitals, it will. Bears cannot be stopped by a human hand strategically placed over an area. Best case scenario is you die with no face, no genitals, and no hands.

Nobody wants to die looking like this fool.

Mistake #2:

Screaming

There is nothing manly about screaming.

A bear can take many of things from you, such as your eyes, head, organs, and legs. One thing they can't take is your dignity. You give that up freely when you choose to scream or shriek in a confrontation. Screaming will do nothing but bring your family shame. If you must make noise while confronting the bear, try shouting obscenities and cutting insults at the animal.

Mistake #3: Going for the Eyes

Many people think a bear can be blinded if its eyes are stabbed or scooped out with a spoon. Bears do not need their eyes because they see with their heart. Taking out the eyes is useless in a bear confrontation.

Bears see with their hearts, not their eyes.

Mistake #4:
Calling for the Rangers

People place a lot of false security in forest rangers. In truth, rangers are just

humans with funny hats. There is nothing they can do that you cannot do yourself. The only thing a ranger can do is update the park's "Days Since a Bear Attack" sign, and that rarely changes from zero.

Rangers only provide mythical safety.

Mistake #5: Don't Make It About Winning

The biggest mistake people make when fighting a bear is making it all about winning. You aren't in this to win, you are in it for the fight. Think small. Get

in a few good shots, try to come up with a cool catchphrase, do something awesome. You are going to die, that's a given. Think about how you want to be remembered and put the idea of winning out of your mind.

There is freedom in embracing bear death.

BEAR SPRAY AND OTHER LIES

There is an entire industry that thrives on the false belief that bear attacks can be stopped or even prevented. Similar to other unregulated "miracle" products that make wild claims, like diet pills, hypnosis, exercise, and organic food, bear prevention products and handbooks are a waste of time and money. Much like the way big tobacco was once able to make outrageous claims that cigarettes were healthy and could cure cancer, the bear attack prevention industry will one day be seen for the sham that it is. These gimmicks and ploys feed the insecurity of those who want to wear rose-colored glasses in a world facing the insurmountable obstacle of bear aggression. While the emotion behind these desires is only human, so is the fate of mankind. Bears are going to kill us, and no sprays, traps, platitudes, firepower, or atomic bombs have come close to changing that fact.

Let's take a look at some of the bear attack prevention industry's most reckless and unsubstantiated lies, from products to just plain bad advice.

Lie #1: *Bear Spray*

One of the most popular bear prevention products on the market is bear spray. There is nothing more appealing than the idea that with just a small amount of mist shot out of an easy-to-carry aerosol can, one can send a bear running back into the forest snorting and sneezing with tears in its eyes. Unfortunately, bears are not mosquitos. You cannot simply spritz the problem away. Rather than ward off attacks, bear spray often has the opposite effect. The chemicals in most bear sprays increase the bear's rage and invite a more angry, violent attack.

Here's one way to get a guaranteed laugh out of a bear.

USE BEAR SPRAY TO ANGER THE BEAR

YOU ARE GOING TO DIE ANYWAY, AND AN ANGRY BEAR WILL KILL YOU FASTER

We had six of our top product testers spray a bear in the face with leading brands of bear spray. Of course, they all died, but who died fastest for the price?

There are a lot of bear sprays on the market these days, and all of them claim they can protect you from bears. While that is absolutely false, some of them will get you killed more slowly than others. When buying bear spray, you want a product that will anger the bear enough to kill you quickly. Nobody wants to die a slow death. When our six product testers put their own lives on the line, they chose these six name brand bear sprays.

Though we could not interview our product testers due to their being slain in the process, we did gather a lot of valuable information. Surprisingly, Bear Away™, the lowest-priced bear spray currently on the market, was the most effective, causing the quickest and most painless death. Next was Ursine Mist®, a fragrant spray derived from human urine which claims to also attract human females, but was the most expensive brand available. Surprisingly, despite being 98% hydrochloric acid, Grizzle Drizzle© was not as effective, leaving the victim to spend over three seconds in agony before finally passing on. Cub Splash™, a bear spray marketed to kids, angered the bear, but it took much longer for the tester to be slain. After that, Bear Off!™, Grizz Repel©, and Hey Bear!® all ranked dismally, taking multiple minutes for the tester to die, with the worst of all leaving the product tester to be slowly and casually torn at for nearly two weeks.

Bear spray is useful if your goal is to piss off a bear so much that it wants to kill you, but you should know what you're getting yourself into before you buy. **Full analysis on next page.**

IN MEMORY OF OUR DEDICATED PRODUCT
TESTING STAFF:

Timothy McGuire 1952-2017
Paul Donahue 1955-2017
Clive O'Reilly 1989-2017
Mary-Beth MacWilliams 1962-2017
Frank Mutton 1984-2017
Wolfgang Van Giordanio 1982-2017
Mark McKinney 1952-2017

Top Bear Spray Comparison

BEAR AWAY Large animal repellent	**Brand:** Bear Away™ **Price:** $4.99 **Active ingredient:** *DEET* **Time to Death (TTD):** *0.02 seconds* **Bear Rage Level (BRL):** *10* ***Consumer Rating:*** *Unknown due to death of tester*
Ursine Mist repellant & cologne	**Brand:** Bear Away™ **Price:** $21.99 **Active ingredient:** *Human Urine* **Time to Death (TTD):** *0.02 seconds* **Bear Rage Level (BRL):** *10* ***Consumer Rating:*** *Unknown due to death of tester*
Cub Splash bear resistance mist	**Brand:** Cub Splash™ **Price:** $8.85 **Active ingredient:** *Picaridin* **Time to Death (TTD):** *22.3 seconds* **Bear Rage Level (BRL):** *8* ***Consumer Rating:*** *Unknown due to death of tester*
Bear Off! long-lasting bear protection	**Brand:** Bear Off!™ **Price:** $7.75 **Active ingredient:** *Oil of Lemon Eucalyptus* **Time to Death (TTD):** *3:23 minutes* **Bear Rage Level (BRL):** *5* ***Consumer Rating:*** *Unknown due to death of tester*
Grizzle Drizzle bear spray	**Brand:** Grizzle Drizzle© **Price:** $7.99 **Active ingredient:** *Hydrochloric acid* **Time to Death (TTD):** *3.7 seconds* **Bear Rage Level (BRL):** *9* ***Consumer Rating:*** *Unknown due to death of tester*
Grizz Repel anti-bear assualt spray	**Brand:** Grizz Repel© **Price:** $11.25 **Active ingredient:** *IR3535* **Time to Death (TTD):** *8:28 minutes* **Bear Rage Level (BRL):** *3* ***Consumer Rating:*** *Unknown due to death of tester*
HEY, BEAR! ursine dismissal agent	**Brand:** Hey Bear!® **Price:** $6.95 **Active ingredient:** *Novelty fart spray* **Time to Death (TTD):** *12 days, 13 hours, 19 minutes* **Bear Rage Level (BRL):** *1* ***Consumer Rating:*** *Unknown due to death of tester*

Lie #2: If It's Brown, Lie Down

People often think that just because something rhymes then it must be true. You should never do something just because it rhymes, especially lie down in a bear attack. Not only is it lazy, but it's an embarrassing way to die. Whatever color the bear is, the stupidest thing you can do is attempt to take a nap. Lying down in a bear attack is nothing more than last-minute death practice.

Lying down in a bear attack is great practice for being dead, which is about to happen anyway.

Lie #3: If It's Black, Fight Back

Again with the rhymes. Don't let this clever wordsmithery make you think for one second that if a black bear attacks you, fighting back will somehow enhance your chances of survival. Fighting back is always an option, no matter what color the bear's fur is. The one thing that is not an option is surviving. So go ahead, if it's white, fly a kite. If it's red, bake it bread. If it's green, play tambourine. If it's a bear, you're dead.

Bear fighting is a good way to die like a man, no matter the color of its fur.

Lie #4: *A Fed Bear Is a Dead Bear*

And yet another rhyme that is clearly false. How about this? Rhyming bear advice sounds nice, but if you take it you'll pay the price. Obviously a fed bear is the opposite of a dead bear. A fed bear is a very much alive bear. Bears eat constantly. If a fed bear was a dead bear, I wouldn't be writing this book right now. The truth is, this saying started with a greedy hunter who convinced his companions that the only way to ward off bears was to leave out their best snacks, which he would then eat.

Doesn't look dead to me.

Lie #5: *Bears Only Attack When Provoked*

Who even does this? You probably have met a lot of humans. How many of them have walked out into the forest and poked a bear in the chest and repeatedly called it a lily-livered little punk who needed to be taught a lesson? Never? Exactly, because nobody does that. And yet bear attacks are as common as sunsets. Do the math: bears attack whenever the hell they damn well please.

This ends pretty much as expected.

Lie #6: Try to Make Yourself Appear Bigger

This is one of those concepts that should be met with ridicule the moment it is suggested. If making yourself bigger was an option, there wouldn't be a problem with people not fitting into clothes or getting on carnival rides. It is scientifically impossible to make yourself bigger (except by consuming lots of bundt cake, but no bear is going to wait for that). Even if it's possible to make yourself *appear* bigger, not even the greatest illusionist on earth can make themselves appear bigger than a bear.

While it's not possible to look like a bigger human, it is possible to look like a bigger idiot.

Lie #7: Bop It on the Nose

There is some legitimacy to this advice, but it is not going to help you survive. The bear's nose is the softest part of their face, so if you choose to punch a bear, punch it in the nose. The hard skull of a bear will shatter your fist into tiny, mushy fragments on impact, then you will be torn to pieces. Nobody wants to add a busted hand to an already grisly death. Punch the bear in the nose so that you can go to your death with the pride of having been one of the few humans who decked a bear but didn't die with a broken hand.

Punch a bear in the nose so you don't break your hand on its skull before it inevitably kills you.

Lie #9: Beards Protect You From Bears

Despite many scientific claims to the contrary, having a large beard will not aid you in surviving a bear encounter. Nobody really knows where this myth got its start. Some believe it started with the myths of bearded bear killers like Grizzly Addams, Davy Crockett, and Zangief. These tall tales are fictions perpetrated by the beard oil industry. The fact is if you have a beard and use beard oil to groom it, you are probably attracting more bears than you are fending off. Bears can't stand lumbersexuals with their skinny jeans and fake beards.

Your beard cannot hide your weakness.

Lie #10: Bear Meat

A person who claims to have eaten bear meat is either a pathological liar or suffers from a clinical mental illness known as Ursomastical Dysphoria.

If you think you are eating a bear, you are eating something dead, but it ain't no bear.

Some even go so far as to stuff fake bear costumes and place them in their dens and claim that the meat they have in their freezer came from a bear. Besides the fact that no blade of man can cut through the flesh of a bear, even if you did manage to cut through a bear's muscles using an alien metal known as xiphodiustigorgitrum 3 (the only known bear-cutting metal), the bear meat would instantly heal around the blade and cause it to implode. Next time someone tells you they have eaten bear meat, do them a favor and call the insane asylum on their behalf.

Lie #11: The Right to Bear Arms

While many cite the right to bear arms as god-given, the fact is nobody has the right to bear arms. Even bears do not have arms, they only have front legs and back legs. Bears could claim they have a right to a pair of arms so that they have a centaur-like physique, but bears don't spend their lives griping and moaning about not getting things they were never entitled to in the first place and will probably never have. That's a human trait.

If bears had arms, we'd be even more screwed.

Lie #12:

Does a Bear [Expletive] in the Woods?

Obviously a bear does its business anywhere it pleases. It may be in the woods, in your living room, swinging from a flying helicopter, or on the smoldering ashes of a once-vibrant community. Yes, bears defecate everywhere, though the bear's favorite pastime is projectile crapping into space. Most debris and rocks in space are made up of bear dung that was sent from their rocket-powered anal cannons. Bears can fire waste from their anus with the force of a ten-ton piston.

Another question that is rarely asked: Does a bear break wind in the woods? Absolutely. Bear flatulence is one of the most prevalent causes of mass deforestation and the rapid extinction of wildlife.

While many believe polar bears are victims of global warming, in truth it is they who are blowing holes in the ozone with projectile poop blasts.

Lie #12: *Guns*

Many people claim to have shot bears with guns and killed them. Much like those who claim to have partaken of bear meat, these people are highly delusional and either live a rich fantasy life or suffer from a mental disorder known as Ursine Murder Derangment Syndrome (UMDS). Those who suffer UMDS often tell detailed stories of seeking, hunting, cleaning, stuffing, and even eating a bear. They can recall every detail as if it really happened, despite the fact that every detail is a complete fabrication.

In truth, bears cannot be hit by bullets. Bears see reality at a much higher speed than we do and can see things coming before we even know they have happened. They knew Donald Trump was going to be president way back in the '80s. They can see bullets coming years before they ever exit the gun. Bears can dodge bullets with ease, and will even jump on top of bullets and surf on them when they are in the mood.

*It's a great idea to shoot at a bear if your goal is to see
it jump over the bullet and kill you.*

Chapter 9
Bear Species and Fake Bears

NOT ALL BEARS ARE CREATED EQUAL. That is to say, not all bears are actually bears. True bears are shape-shifting beasts who can alter their size, fur color, and markings on command. While some fur colors are preferred over others (they like brown and black, for reasons we have not yet figured out), they can wear any color they please if they are true bears. Throughout history, mankind has incorrectly identified bears that physically look different as separate species—in fact, all "true" bears are part of the same species. For instance, black bears, polar bears, grizzly bears, and brown bears are all true bears wearing different fur colors and taking on different body shapes.

Fake bears are any animal or object labeled "bear" but having nothing to do with true bears. Koala bears, panda bears, and bearcats are all examples of fake bears. Let's take a detailed look at many examples of true bears.

COMMONLY KNOWN BEAR SPECIES

Brown Bears

One of the most common bear types is the brown bear. The reason bears often choose to wear brown fur is unknown, though humans associate the color brown with pleasing things like chocolate, coffee, and pudding. Brown also works well for blending into forests and muddy areas.

Brown bears are brown.

Black bears are black.

Black Bears

Black bears are the ninjas of the bear kingdom. These bears choose to wear black so that they can blend into the shadows and perform stealth attacks. They also wear black for the same reasons Johnny Cash wore black, but the complete opposite of that.

Grizzly/Kodiak Bears

According to mainstream zoology, grizzlies and kodiaks are considered the largest and most dangerous of the bears. While there are much larger, much more dangerous bears, these are the ones most commonly seen by humans and the shape most commonly taken when bears are on the offensive.

It is believed that bears choose this form because it is the largest size a bear can be and still convince human biologists that they are not aliens or part god (in truth, bears are demigods from an alien planet).

Grizzly bears are classified as mammals but are actually demigods from space.

Polar Bears

Polar bears choose to wear white fur because they think it is superior. They are the KKK of the bear kingdom, making them one of the most horrible bear types. While they could alter their fur color at any moment, polar bears stay white because they think that is the fur color that God intended bears to have.

Bears who wear exclusively white fur are not just vicious, they're bigots.

Spirit Bear

Many Native Americans worshipped the Great Bear Spirit. In truth, bear spirits (or spirit bears) are simply kung fu master bears who can become completely spectral on demand. Spirit bears can enter into human bodies and take control of them at will. This extraordinary ability is why bears show up in one aspect or another in many different world religions.

If a spirit bear seems to be guiding you, it is probably leading you to certain death.

Sloth Bear

The sloth bear is the drunken Nick Nolte of bears. It can barely walk. It wakes up in strange places like apartment lobbies, crashed convertibles, and outside convenience stores covered in blood from people it doesn't remember slaying, finding strange messages tattooed onto its skin, and hair shaved in strange places. The sloth bear is one of the most vicious bears because it takes things incredibly personally. If you get an angry phone call in the middle of the night from a sloth bear, even if it begins to claim it loves you, this dysfunctional creature is sure to lash out at any moment.

Sloth bears are the drunken Nick Nolte of bears.

Asian Black Bear

All asian black bears witnessed their parents being gunned down by muggers outside of a theater one night, and have since decided to stalk the shadows wearing the shaved emblem of a bat on their chest, killing anyone who slightly resembles those who shot all of their parents.

This is the original Batman.

Sun Bears

Sun bears choose to dwell in slightly smaller bodies but have giant, long tongues solely so that they can make hilarious faces. Most sun bears are either uncles, creepy guys, or rock stars. They are called sun bears because they worship the sun and think the world will end in 2020.

Even other bears are creeped out by sun bears.

Spectacled Bear

Spectacled bears are the snobbiest of the bear types. They color their fur in the shape of glasses and then demand they be called spectacles. They like to use big words and never shut up about how they eat exclusively vegan people.

The spectacled bear thinks it's smarter than you and if you try to argue with it, it has some stuff you should read.

Water Bear (Tardigrade)

The tardigrade is a megafauna water bear capable of shifting its size rapidly.

Its face is almost entirely dominated by its hose-shaped mouth, which it uses to suck up prey like a vacuum cleaner, inhaling entire civilizations and defecating them into piles of glowing green mush.

Tardigrades are thought to be the alien mothers of the bear species.

Water bears are known for their ability to survive in deep space, atomic blasts, and extreme temperatures. They can survive extreme pressures and radioactive emissions that would kill all other species. They do not need oxygen to breathe.

While they can survive without food for centuries, it is in their nature to kill without ceasing. Tardigrades can wipe out thousands of people or animals within minutes. They have six chubby legs that move slowly but can crush or climb over any surface.

They use telepathic communication to formulate global attacks. Scientists guess these creatures came from another world and are the alien mother of the bear species.

Though they often take their microscopic form, tardigades are capable of becoming larger than planets in the blink of an eye.

LESSER-KNOWN BEAR SPECIES

There are many bear species so deadly that they have never been featured on National Geographic and have been banned from *Ranger Rick* for their disturbing appearances. Most scientists who have attempted to study these bears have died in the process, so very little is known about them. Also, unlike other animals, bears can reproduce with any species, giving birth to any variety of abominations.

The male Bearboon has a second set of enormous testicles located in its butt region.

Bearboon

The bearboon is usually found hiding in the grasslands of Africa. The tall grass makes it easier for the bearboon to stalk prey, focusing mostly on people riding in safari jeeps wearing little round hats.

The bearboon's howl is so powerful that, when directed at an unsuspecting person or animal, their flesh will be blown off, leaving behind only blood and bones.

The most shocking aspect of the bearboon is its giant reddish-purple booty. Though it cannot harm you, it is of no comfort that if the bearboon devours you, its horrible chewing-gum anus will be your only means of escape.

The San Diego Zoo once opened a bearboon exhibit. Many, many people died.

The bearantula is the main reason the Pegasus is now an endangered species.

Bearantula

The bearantula has eight large and hairy legs, six eyes, and can see in all directions. It uses sharp upper teeth to chew its food, while it has two massive bear claws as lower teeth that hang from their mouths. These "handibles" are used to catch prey and stuff it into their crunching mouth hole.

The bearantula has a strong proclivity for the flavor of Pegasus meat. They build giant webs to capture the flying steeds, then bind them up like mummies. The creature then inserts its proboscis into its prey that emits an innard-liquefying acid, then sucks the bloody stew back out of its prey, leaving behind a hollow, bony husk. They are commonly found in stables and barns.

Bearwhal

The bearwhal is often called the unicorn of the bear species due to the large horns they have on their foreheads. The bearwhals use this horn in both hunting and mating rituals. Bearwhals hunt in groups, spearing their prey

The bearwhal can shishkebab entire snorkeling teams.

by impaling them with their horns. Their most common prey include the Arctic Cod and the Greenland Halibut, with scuba divers and mermaids often being victims as well.

Beargle

A pure-beared beargle.

A beargle is a very large species of canine bear. It sports black, white, and brown fur, with large floppy ears, a keen nose, and eyes all askew.

The beargle attacks by biting your calves and thighs, causing you to fall down, where it will proceed to chomp off your feet. The beargle does this to humans, cows, and large species of birds, such as ostriches and swans.

The male beargle will sometimes kill his own cubs if he feels they are looking at him funny.

Other Beargle

The Beargle Effect: Every time it flaps its wings, a hurricane happens everywhere.

The other kind of beargle is part bear, part eagle. It was briefly the symbol of freedom in a country that was soon after wiped out by that very symbol they so cherished, and has since been completely forgotten.

Beargles feed mostly on airliners and the few remaining pterodactyls. While some people think the flap of a butterfly wing could potentially cause a hurricane in another part of the world, the beargle's wings cause hurricanes every time they flap, without question.

A beargle can see its prey at any distance. It has the ability to zoom in on anything and increase the resolution of a picture if needed, simply by shouting, "Enhance image!"

The octobear can fit through any hole, even minor plot holes.

Octobear

The octobear has eight large tentacles that can crush bones into powder with one twist. Their skeleton can become malleable, giving them the ability to fit through tight spaces. They have numerous tactics for attacking prey, including the expulsion of hydrochloric ink, camouflage, deimatic behavior (shape changing), and a venomous harpoon that emerges from their rectum. Because they can fit through any hole, they have been known to climb into people's bodily orifices and then tear them apart from the inside.

The octobear hunts mostly in dark places. It prefers human meat, but may settle for farm or zoo animals if driven by hunger. Sea-dwelling octobears live mostly on a steady diet of sharks and nuclear submarines.

Bear Crab

The bear crab has been scientifically proven to give people more nightmares than any other creature in existence. It has claws, six pointy legs, and a hard exoskeleton. The bear crab's pincers are incredibly sharp, and have the ability to cut a morbidly obese man completely in half and a small man in thirds.

If you are looking at this, you will have nightmares.

The tribearatops never went extinct because it is part bear.

Tribearatops

Unlike most dinosaurs who went extinct, the Tribearatops causes other species to go extinct. While it is working on the extinction of mankind, it passes the time wiping out other creatures such as purple penguins, three-legged frogs, and red-crested basset hounds. Poachers have often sought out the tribearatops in hopes of cutting off their horns to sell the ivory, but have all died, which has made triberatops ivory even more valuable (that's basic economics). One tribearatops horn is worth so much, it could pay off the U.S. national debt multiple times.

Bear Bat/Bearodactyl

The nocturnal bear bat cannot see well in light and has sensitive ears that can follow the echoes of their roars. This creature sleeps in caves or hollowed out buildings while hanging upside-down. Bear bats hunt at night—mostly for humans—using sonar or searching for the glow of their iPhones. The prey is carried back to their cave, where the whole colony will participate in the feast.

If a superhero dressed as a bear bat, criminals would immediately find new jobs.

Star-Nosed Mole-Bear

The star-nosed mole-bear has generally poor eyesight, but the large pink appendages on their snouts work simultaneously as visual, auditory, and olfactory receptors, and even as a cool mustache. These creatures dig massive tunnels underground and can tear through almost anything. They get their sustenance by bursting from the ground and snapping up passers by with their large teeth. Despite their large size, star-nosed mole-bears are very sneaky. Over time, they have made tunnels throughout the Earth's crust that lead almost everywhere, enabling other bear species to travel beneath us unseen.

Star-nosed mole-bears often dig beneath brick walls to give other bears a route behind guarded areas.

Bearmadillo

The bearmadillo is covered in armor formed by dermal bones. They have very short legs, with long claws that are like butcher knives which can cut a human to pieces easily. They move very fast, and can also roll up into a ball and break through anything. If a rolling boulder and bearmadillo crash into each other at full force, the bearmadillo will win.

These creatures are easily set off by "What's the bearma-dilly-o" jokes.

Grizzly Boar

The grizzly boar is the most aggressive of all urswine hybrids. Its tusks can rip a person in half from top to bottom. It lives in arid regions, often fashioning caves out of piles of bones to keep cool. Males emit an odor that causes immediate vomiting of blood, followed by death. The odor secretes from a gland in the humps on their backs, where urine and bile mix to form a pungent, deadly, sinus-melting acid. It is not to be confused with the grizzly *bore*, which is a grizzly that just keeps talking about itself at parties.

The most aggressive of urswine beasts.

Bearnoceros

The bearnoceros cannot see well, so it relies on its sense of smell to seek and destroy prey such as villagers, deer, zebras, and large birds. While rhino horns are useful for medicinal purposes, bearnoceros horns leak a type of toxin that causes you to feel a burning sensation in your pelvic region for the remainder of your short, agony-filled life.

The bearnoceros always prefers its full name be used. Never call it a "bearno."

FAKE BEARS

There are many animals and even inanimate objects that have stolen the "bear" moniker. These misleading charlatans should never be called "bears."

Koala "Bears"
Even if they drop on people and murder them, koalas are not bears. They look more like Mickey Mouse parrot sloths.

Panda "Bears"
Not bears. Giant lazy raccoons.

Gummy "Bears"
While there are real gummy bears, the candy ones you can buy at the movies are fake bears.

Teddy Bears
Though useful for bear propaganda, teddy bears are in no way actual bears and are horrible guests at tea parties.

Bearcat
The bearcat is neither of the animals it purports to be, but is rather some kind of large muskrat weasel.

Red Panda
The red panda is not even a panda, let alone a bear. It is a raccoon that originally came from Scotland.

Chapter 10

Bear News:
True Stories That Went Unreported

HISTORY IS FULL OF LIES, and as President Trump says, the news is often fake. This is true for any subject matter, but few subjects have been so misconstrued in our lexicon of published knowledge as the many lies written about bears.

In this chapter, we will take a look at some of the news stories that were either hidden in the back pages of newspapers or never published at all by the mainstream media. Many of these stories were submitted by reputable journalists but mysteriously never saw print. Often, the newspapers, magazines, journals, and websites that were to make these stories public were mysteriously destroyed before the stories saw the light of day.

If it's not obvious, allow me to spell it out: Bears. Bears control the media. In fact, the chances of this book being published at all are very slim. If you currently hold this book in your hands, the good news is that it did see print. The bad news is that your very possession of it puts you at extreme risk.

Enjoy this chapter.

BEAR NEWS YOU PROBABLY MISSED

Bear Kills Cancer Submitted to Utah Herald 12/14/86, never published

In these revolutionary tests, a bear killed a vial full of cancer cells, then everyone else in the room.

It was a cure found by accident when a lone grizzly bear invaded the Bradley Meyer Cancer Research Clinic in Buckley, North Dakota. The beast killed multiple lab workers and turned the place upside-down. However, when the bear cleared out, the evidence it left behind was miraculous.

"Any cancer specimen left behind was tested and the cancer had been killed completely," said surviving researcher Rhonda Scott. Scott immediately began putting together a team to begin bear cancer research. "Everyone knows bears are killing machines, but who knew they could kill cancer too?"

Since research began, 87% of Scott's team has died in testing. "Yes, there is a cure for cancer, but it's unpopular in the medical community because it's bears, and bears kill a ton of doctors." The National Alliance of Physicians has stated that killing multiple doctors off every time cancer needs to be cured is "not worthwhile", but so far no other way has been found.

"The bear won't just kill the cancer. It has to get whipped up into such a blind rage that the cancer can only be a bystander in its rampage of death. If we don't sacrifice at least a few medical staff, we can't get results," Scott said. Scott also stated that the only way to cure a cancer patient using the bear technique was to kill the patient, "which is kind of pointless".

Cancer research still has a long way to go. Some people say bears will be the death of humankind, and they probably will be. But the silver lining would be that cancer might finally be defeated.

Study: Crying Like Pansy Increases Risk of Bear Attack

Originally published in the Lakeside Times, 4/2/96, page 78

Bears are attracted to the salty smell of man tears.

Maybe it really is time to suck it up. A new study from the Center for Science and Factual Information reveals that bears target namby-pamby, lily-livered, yellow-bellied, pantywaist crybabies.

Test results reveal a solid correlation between weeping like a bellyaching little sissy and attracting bear attacks. The evidence seems to indicate that bears have a keen sense for detecting "bitching and moaning like a little puss-cake" and they can't stand "weepy, whiny, puerile twaddle".

Scientists used a variety of test subjects to conduct the research, from people who were crying legitimate tears for lost loved ones to juvenile milksops whimpering and sniveling about vapid B.S. like canceled Netflix series, online romantic entanglements, and dropped ice cream cones.

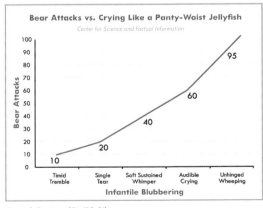

"Bear attack prevention starts with your ability to suck it up and stop being such a little cream puff," says lead researcher Aaron Reiger. "The more you howl and sob over petty drivel, the more likely you are to be a target. So just stop it. Stop. Get over it. What, are you gonna cry? Little baby gonna cry?"

Research Courtesy of Dr. Kyle Riley

211.

GPS Implant Reveals Bears Are Time-Traveling, Trans-Dimensional, Intergalactic Ninjas

Originally submitted to National Geographic, 7/15/2008, unpublished

In June of 2004, researchers at the Center for Ursine Research succeeded in planting a GPS tracker on an Alaskan grizzly. Once tracked, the bear—known to the research team as "Bear 238"—revealed an intergalactic journey of revenge, spanning time and space like no other creature on Earth.

"We knew things were going to get interesting when the bear hijacked a rocket at NASA and forced a team of astronauts to fly him into a wormhole. From there we tracked the bear through various galaxies as it devoured multiple undiscovered life forms and went through a time portal to the 15th Century to kill a man named Hodge. We have no idea why he killed this man because his legacy has been wiped from history," lead research analyst Karl Frumpkins said.

Its mission seemed both calculated and meandering. Sometimes the bear sought sustenance, like when it broke into a Turkish honey factory. Other times it was exacting revenge on humans and animals who apparently had done it wrong. At one point, the bear entered a dojo in ancient Japan and defeated thirty-seven black belt ninjas. Another leg of the journey involved the bear becoming microscopic and entering the bloodstreams of humans, causing an incurable virus called the Ursine Death Flu.

The bear's motivation remains a mystery, and the tracker, which cost researchers $34 million, has little chance of being retrieved.

This bear was tracked all the way from the Smoky Mountain National Forest to this unknown dimension.

THE TOP TEN BEAR FIGHTERS IN HISTORY

Throughout history, men and women—but mostly men—have gone into battle with bears, often knowing full well that they would not come out alive.

This phenomenon of bear fighting began with the Latvian folk hero Lāčplēsis (Bear Slayer), who managed to kick a bear in the face right before it killed him. This was seen as such a brazen and heroic act that Lāčplēsis's legend grew over time, until he was written about in poems and portrayed in sculptures as killing a bear.

This historical sketch shows a man's failed attempt at a bear headlock.

From that point forward, many men have sought to die in the most legendary way possible: fighting a bear. It is a sport that nobody can win. The victory is only in the effort you put into dying awesomely.

In this section, we will take a look at the ten greatest bear fighters in the history of bear fighting.

A young bear slays a hunter and his forty hounds (London, 1545).

Sculpture of Lāčplēsis.

#10 Neal the Drunk and Hungry

Born approx. 852 AD
Died approx. 880 AD

Neal the Drunk was a low-rung Viking mostly known for his heavy drinking habits, belligerence, and massive red beard. Had he not died in a confrontation with thirteen bears, he probably would not have gone down in history as he did.

The brutal Norwegian was also known for his insatiable appetite. Often fueled by drunkenness, Neal would stagger into the woods and eat hares, adders, and foxes raw,

Neal the Drunk and Hungry
(Painting 1200 AD).

often chewing on them as they remained kicking in his mouth. However, one night Neal's drunken appetite raged so hard that, despite the many warnings against it, he decided he wanted to taste bear.

After three days of binging on beer and trekking through the Norwegian wilderness, Neal came upon a ravine with thirteen brown bears rummaging among countless skeletal remains of humans, moose, and other creatures. Driven by hunger, Neal dove into the pit and landed on top of one of the bears. He managed to bite off a quarter-inch piece of bear ear before he was torn into many pieces. He died doing what he loved: fulfilling his dream of tasting bear. His final words: "Tastes like murder chicken."

Archaeologists believe these bones, found in a ravine in a Norway forest,
may have belonged to Neal the Drunk and Hungry.

#9 Joshua "Judo" Rice

Born: 8/12/1980
Died: 11/22/2014

Joshua Rice, from Las Vegas, Nevada, began studying judo at four months old. By age nine, he was a quadruple black belt judo master. Having mastered American judo, Rice went on to study judo in Japanese jungles with the descendants of Kanō Jigorō, the creator of judo. This secret society would fight indigenous wildlife such as spider crabs, snow monkeys, and giant salamanders. The only animal the clan forbade confronting was the Ussuri

Rice perches on a cliff side in Sweden's Norrland region.

Brown Bear. Rice defeated every other animal in Japan but wanted badly to prove himself against a bear.

Not wanting to dishonor his clansmen, Rice went on a pilgrimage into remote areas of Sweden to test his judo against Swedish brown bears. Rice got into a judo bout with an 800-pound brown bear deep in the Norrland region. During the fight, Rice performed one of the most difficult judo throws on the bear, the Sumi-Otoshi. Even though it turned out that the bear was allowing him to do this move so that it could transition into a piledriver in midair, this remains the most impressive attempt ever at using judo against a bear.

Sumi-Otoshi Vs. Bear *Nobody has ever pulled off all five steps against a bear.*

#8 Dave "Big Papa" Hesse

Born: 10/27/1858

Died: 1/30/1915

Big Papa Dave Hesse lived in a massive five-story log cabin in Kadenbrielle, Tennessee with 302 orphans of bear-slain families. He built the cabin with the help of his pet bear, Zeke. The only thing bigger than Hesse's cabin was his heart.

Unfortunately, the bear Zeke was a false ally who had only aided Hesse so that his bear friends could come and finish the job they had started with the orphans' parents. One day, forty bears descended on the cabin to devour the orphans.

Papa Dave Hesse, Shoshone National Forest, 1913.

Hesse, always ready for anything, sent the children into an underground coal mine to escape in a system of track carts. But one child, Josiah DeLaney, had been separated from the others and was in danger. Josiah, being a small child, was eaten by one of the larger grizzlies. Hesse immediately doused himself with salmon fat so that the bear would swallow him quickly and cleanly. Once inside, Hesse blasted a hole through the bear's rib cage with his shotgun, pushing Josiah out, saving him but ultimately sacrificing himself.

Hesse's log cabin orphanage for children of the Ursine War*.

Today, Hesse's cabin has become a monument to bear fighting, curated by DeLaney's daughter, Rachel. Visitors can see the variety of skins and pelts from Hesse's collection, as well as watch a dramatic reenactment of the day he saved Josiah DeLaney.

*Though humans named this event the Ursine War, for bears it was simply a casual outing to acquire snacks. A true bear war would wipe out all humans completely.

#7 Carl "Collapsed Earth" Allen

Born: 4/14/1964
Died: 1/24/2017

As a Southern California pipeline construction manager, Carl Allen—commonly referred to as "Al"—was not someone people would assume would go down in the annals of bear fighting history. The biggest events in Carl's life had been the construction of large diameter (6-to-12 feet) pipelines and tunnels. When his crew inadvertently dug their way into the nest of a star-nosed mole bear, all of that changed.

Carl Allen (not a bear).

Al soon realized that the mole bear had been digging out tunnels for other bears, giving them easy access to people's homes and places of work. The creature was creating a matrix of secret pathways for bears to pop up from the ground like gophers and attack their prey.

Since his boss didn't believe his story, Al took matters into his own hands. He hijacked a number of fuel trucks and poured high-octane fuel into the bear's system of tunnels, then lit it on fire. The resulting explosion caved in the tunnels and caused the earth in the area to sink thirteen feet, collapsing multiple buildings.

Al was later found and killed by bears. What he did to slow down their underground network of murder tunnels temporarily saved countless lives, but most people were just mad at him for the traffic inconvenience he caused.

One of the areas affected by Carl's subterranean explosion.

#6 Eric "Hell Ripper" Porter

Born: 1002 AD

Died: 1039 AD

Eric Porter was the legendary warrior/hunter who led the band of Irish warriors known as the Decapitators, famous for slaying multiple giants in the marshes of their home country.

Porter first came to prominence after catching and eating the Salmon of Vengeance from the River Slaney. He was able to capture the salmon because Ireland's bear population was low at the time. Most bears were so busy eating leprechauns that they failed to guard their sacred river. Upon ingesting this mystical fish, Porter gained the ability to slice through bears like warm butter with his sword, which he called "Ifreann Sracadh" (Hell Ripper).

Porter's acquisition of the salmon attracted every bear in Ireland to his location, where his gang of giant slayers was easily defeated. However,

"Legend of Hell Ripper" woodcut, 1213 A.D.

Porter managed to slice the bears into pieces using a rapid slicing technique known as banshee blade, which rendered the animals into what amounted to seventeen piles of ground bear-beef. Days later, Porter died of the "Bearbonic Plague," a disease caused by the thousands of microscopic bears that resulted from Porter's blade, since bear pieces always rapidly regenerate. Other plagues in Ireland, such as the Black Death, can be traced back to this incident. Still, Porter remains the only man in history to cut multiple bears into tiny pieces... though he probably shouldn't have done that.

Depiction of Bearbonic Plague, 1040 A.D.

#5 Jeffrey "The Hiker" Kranz

Born: 7/14/1981
Died: 6/4/2011

Though he was the multi-billion dollar founder of Kranz Ketchup-Flavored Syrup, Jeffrey Kranz was known to his friends and family as a silent, solitary man who enjoyed interacting with the wilderness more than human beings. Kranz would often go on solo hikes for weeks at a time.

However, on his final outing into Yosemite National Park, Kranz found himself face-to-face with a 1,700-pound brown bear. Instead of trying to escape, Kranz lunged down the bear's throat, forcing the bear to swallow him whole. Kranz went on to text his only friend from

Kranz, the day he left for Yosemite.

inside the bear. He survived inside of the bear, sending texts, for two weeks.

Part of the text conversation Kranz sent his friend, E-Money Adams, from the inside of a bear.

Kranz survived on whatever the bear ate. He carved a small hole out of the bear's ribs using a ballpoint pen. He used this opening to get air and to try to see where the bear was headed. Because Kranz was blocking the bear's digestive system, the bear did not defecate for nearly fourteen days.

At one point during the bear's constipated journey, Kranz realized the bear was approaching a troop of Boy Scouts. Kranz shouted a warning through his peephole at the campers, and then he began devouring the bear's organs from the inside.

Unfortunately, Kranz's immune system didn't react well to the consumption of uncooked bear organs, and he died from salmonella poisoning. His death is a grim reminder of the importance of blow-torching the inside of a bear before you consume it.

#4 Jairus "Kill Slam" Pascale

Born: December 6, 1968
Died: August 27th, 1994

Legendary wrestler Jairus Pascale (known in the ring as "Kill Slam") announced his desire to fight bears after winning his seventeenth consecutive belt in the WWC. He announced his plan to release four bears into the ring at once, himself at the center with only a sword and a folding chair as weapons. The ropes would be lit on fire, and the death metal band Extol would perform over the proceedings.

Most predicted that this would be a death match for Pascale, and they were correct. But Pascale went

Jairus "Kill Slam" Pascale.

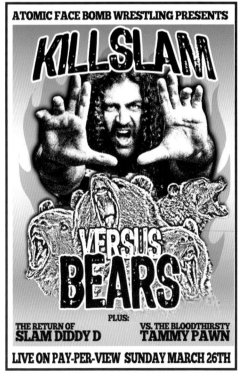

Poster for the event that ended Pascale's career and life.

in well aware of his fate. "I accept this match not to defeat bears, but to dominate men." Depending upon whom you talk to, Jairus did just that.

In the brief cage match, Jairus was turned into a cloud of blood within moments of the four bears being let into the ring. However, slow-motion video reveals that Jairus performed 67% of a suplex on one of the bears before he was killed. Many wrestlers have attempted this since and have not even come close. In the wrestling community, people who gamble on these bear death matches with wrestlers trying to beat Kill Slam's record refer to the challenge as "Pascale's Wager."

#3 Jon "BEAR H@ck3r" Fenton

Born: May 14, 1944

Died: March 3, 1987

Jon Fenton worked in the IT department of a top secret animal aggression biology lab in San Jose in the '80s. During this period, Fenton became adept at animal hacking—finding digital connections into the brains of animals, harnessing their aggression, and turning it into information. He once downloaded the entire mind of a sloth onto one thousand 5-1/4" floppy disks. Decoding revealed that the sloth's entire

Fenton was arguably the greatest hacker in the '80s.

psyche was obsessed with the pain it experienced while pooping, as well as the fear of pooping again. This was a revolutionary discovery.

However, when Fenton decided to hack into a Eurasian Brown Bear, he met his match. At first, the download seemed to be going well, but then suddenly every computer in a forty-mile radius got the Blue Screen of Death. An image of a bear appeared on the screens, and thousands of Silicon Valley residents were sucked into their computers and trapped in heavily-encrypted folders. Fenton responded by doubling down on his efforts and trying to send a virus into the bear that would turn its mind into a neverending succession of ASCII art spam. The bear exploded and thousands of lives were saved.

Fenton's computer was found with this bear hack still on the screen.

Later that day, when Fenton logged onto one of his home computers, he realized that he had been hacked by bears. Moments later, he was mauled to death.

#2 Dr. Paul "Psycho-Plastic" Auerbach

Born: May 13, 1965

Died: February 12, 2018

Renowned plastic surgeon Dr. Paul Auerbach of Los Angeles was known for his eccentricity and willingness to take on any plastic surgery request, legal or not. From run-of-the-mill facelifts to transplanting limbs onto people's foreheads, there was no task Dr. Paul was too sane to take on. However, the most exceptional transplant Auerbach ever accomplished was transplanting a human face onto a bear.

Dr. Paul Auerbach was a madman with a scalpel.

After getting its face ripped off in a salmon peeler, a bear found its way to Auerbach's office, threatening through growls and grunts that if he didn't give the bear a new face, it would kill everyone in Los Angeles. Auerbach accepted the challenge, using the corpse of one of the bear's victims as a donor (a man in the waiting area who was there to get his tongue elongated). After seventeen hours of painstaking surgery, Auerbach transplanted the face, and the bear left the building with a brand new countenance. It was the first human-bear-face transplant (urso-homoplasty) in history.

The bear had no idea it would be getting a human face. Furious, it killed Auerbach immediately after the surgery. Surprisingly, however, the bear spared Los Angeles because the new face it was wearing itched severely. Auerbach, knowing that bears are extremely allergic to soy-based foods, had hidden a layer of vegan cheese slices under the bear's new face. The bear ended up scratching the face off on cacti in the Palm Desert and suffered lifelong burning and deformity because of the soy, which has a hydrochloric acid-like effect on bears.

The historic face transplant.

222.

#1 Dickinson Killdeer

Born: ?

Many say Dickinson Killdeer is a myth. Killdeer is the only man on record who has killed multiple actual bears and lived to tell of it. While there is no known photographic or video evidence of Killdeer fighting bears, the few eyewitnesses who claim to have been rescued by him say his preferred methods of defense are punching, elbowing, and stabbing.

The only known photograph of Dickinson Killdeer as an adult.

His preferred weapons are a knife cut from stone, a hand-made chopping maul, bow and arrow, and spears.

Killdeer's past is unknown, but many believe the tattered Boy Scout kerchief he wears around his neck is proof that he was once a Boy Scout who got lost in the forest, perhaps the only survivor of a mass bear attack.

Others believe Killdeer somehow became part bear during his time in the forest. Unlike other humans, Killdeer seems able to predict a bear's moves before it makes them. Some even believe he can hear their thoughts

While it has never been confirmed, Killdeer scholars believe that the child circled in this photograph could be a young Dickinson Killdeer. This entire troop was eaten by bears. When authorities identified the remains, they found remnants from every troop member except for Killdeer's.

and communicate with them telepathically. Witnesses claim he carries raw salmon in his fur vest and eats it whole, much like a bear.

One survivor was part of a environmental activism group devoted to saving the trees. This woman claimed she and a large group of other activists chained themselves to several trees as part of a protest. The leader of the group swallowed the only padlock key to prevent loggers from removing them from the area. Unfortunately, the group became trapped in the forest all night, and by morning realized they were being targeted by bears. According to the witness, Dickinson Killdeer arrived, helped them cut the chains, and took out a number of bears using only a crudely formed ax, bow and arrow, and his fists.

Killdeer's whereabouts remain a mystery. Government agencies have sent out entire squadrons to search the forests of America to locate him, in hopes that he could be the general who would lead the American military in the coming war against bears. So far, Killdeer has only been seen by those he has rescued. Many believe he was never found because—if Killdeer is part bear as some believe—he likely would have been hibernating during this time. It's also possible that, much like bears, Killdeer is a master of stealth and is only seen by those he allows.

Whatever the case, Killdeer's "rural legend" has permeated American culture, much like Paul Bunyan, Johnny Appleseed, or Pee-Wee Herman.

Dickinson Killdeer as depicted in the cautionary graphic novel,
BEARMAGEDDON.

Chapter 11
How to Defeat a Bear

YOU CAN'T. Nobody can.

CONCLUSION

In case the title of this book wasn't clear enough, BEARS WANT TO KILL YOU. The thousands of slain researchers who made this book hope that message has been made very clear. If they haven't already, bears will kill you.

Thank you for taking an interest in this fascinating topic. Before we part ways, however, allow me to share a few more tidbits about humankind's inevitable demise.

AFTERWORD

What Now?

An Inevitable Confrontation

You can be sure that at some point you will come face-to-face with a bear. You may be in your car, up a tree, at a church picnic, or reading this very book. At a moment when you least expect it, your time will come.

You may think that some people will survive, that bears can't possibly kill all of us. However, this is precisely what is going to happen. What bears are currently doing—and what they have been up to since mankind began recording their habits—has been only a precursor compared to the ultimate plan that bears have for humanity. They want total human annihilation, not stopping until every human being on this earth has been destroyed and replaced by a bear thriving in its stead.

When people talk about the future, they talk about flying cars.
But the real future will be normal cars destroyed by bears.

BEARMAGEDDON

Even near a "bear crossing" sign, people will not be safe when Bearmageddon comes.

Bears know that they are the true dominant species on Earth. This planet is theirs for the taking, and so they have decided to take it. Little is known about the details of their plot. What little we do know has come from research into bear thought and communication.

Up to this point, the bear plot has been to get us to let down our guard, and to focus our sights on other threats, foreign and domestic. We don't put much thought into bear warfare, and that is how they want it.

Evidence has been mounting that bears have quietly been hijacking military bases to steal weapons and human technology. Nuclear missiles have come up missing, and technicians who work on high-level weaponry have disappeared. While you may think it's obvious that this is all the work of bears, your government doesn't, and so they turn a blind eye.

Nobody knows when Bearmageddon will hit, but even when it does, not one of us will be ready.

THE RUXPIN PROJECT

Much of the information in this book comes courtesy of the Ruxpin Project. Though still in its infancy, the Ruxpin Project seeks to take the thoughts of a bear and translate them into spoken English. By tapping into a bear's brain activity, science has been able to achieve amazing breakthroughs in bear communication.

An intricate system of wires and probes is inserted into the bear's brain and contained inside of a glass helmet that keeps the exposed brain from becoming contaminated. The helmet is outfitted with speakers and a microphone that run through a computer, which translates the incoming and outgoing messages so that the bear can both give and receive communication.

The scientific bear research community dismissed this contraption until a breakthrough occurred during a routine test. Suddenly, from the speakers in the helmet, a robotic voice clearly said the words, "I desire honey." History was made.

Further communications were then attempted. "I want salmon" and "my back itches" were the next sentences uttered. However, not long after the experiment took a frightening turn. One day the bear said, "I desire this planet." It stopped communicating after that.

The first time a bear ever communicated with humans it said, "I desire honey."

THE GORILLA PROPOSITION

Since scientists discovered that bears were going to wipe human life off the face of the earth, many solutions have been proposed to potentially combat the coming defeat. However, every proposal failed horribly when tests were conducted.

A breakthrough came when zoologist Benjamin Gilbert thoughtfully considered for months the Unanswerable Question—who would win in a fight, a bear or a gorilla? This is the number one question mankind has wrestled with for centuries, with no definitive answer yet found. What Gilbert proposed was that, if the species are so evenly matched, could gorillas be enhanced to raise the odds for mankind? If so, could we get gorillas to fight on the side of human beings?

Gilbert proposed a multi-trillion-dollar cyborg-ape program aimed at adding technological enhancements to gorillas, as well as tapping into their brains to control their decisions. These experiments have remained top secret, for fear of animal activist groups trying to expose and thereby end the experiments.

Could gorillas with cybernetic upgrades rescue the human race from extinction at the paws of bears? Who would win in a global fight between bears and gorillas? Nobody knows, but if we have any hope for our own future, we'd better pray that it's the gorillas.

Could gorillas be the answer?

Bear Fighter Honorable Mentions

Amy and Anthony "Mayo" Munoz
The Munoz family of Battleground, WA, attempted to kill a bear by tricking it into eating a vat of mayonnaise. The bear enjoyed the mayonnaise and killed them because they didn't provide any more. It was worth a try.

Kailey "Trombone" Frizzell
Comic book colorist and videogame artist Kailey Frizzell once strapped a rocket launcher to her trombone and fought a gang of bears while playing "When the Saints Go Marching In". She didn't succeed in warding off any of the bears, but it was an impressive act of heroism.

Doug "the Beard" Stewart
Doug Stewart based his life on the theory that if he could grow a large enough beard, no bear would mess with him. It was a good theory, but was ultimately proven wrong.

"Poison" Ivy Johnston
Ivy Johnston was a drummer and a poison manufacturer. She worked as a researcher on this book. She once attempted to poison a family of bears in order to see what effect it would have. The outcome was that it killed her and everyone she loved.

Mike "The Grill" Weber
Known for his popular line of grilling products, Mike Weber was determined to taste barbecued bear. Weber managed to light a bear on fire and spray it with BBQ sauce, and then he jumped on to get a bite. Nobody knows if he ever got the taste he sought.

IN MEMORY OF THOSE WHO GAVE THEIR LIVES RESEARCHING THIS BOOK

In order to gather the material for this book, many, many research team members had to die. Not all were aware of the dangers inherent to this job. It's hard to convince people to research bears up close if they know they will be dead soon. We are sorry for the losses endured, and hope this portion of the book makes up for it.

IN MEMORY OF

Blaž Brenčič

September 12th, 1986 - March 1, 2017

HE FLEW TOO LOW IN BEAR COUNTRY

Blaž Brenčič was a young pilot from Slovenia who was attempting to acquire aerial photographs of bears performing cliff-drop body slams in the forests of Austria. The only way to accomplish this safely was to maintain an altitude of 2,000 feet and use a high-powered lens to capture the animals candidly. However, Brenčič allowed his plane to lose elevation as he was attempting a photograph, and a bear leapt 1,956 feet and volleyball-spiked the plane into a mountainside. Though it can be assumed Brenčič captured some unprecedented images of bears in action, the film was destroyed in the crash.

Brenčič is survived by his wife, Malena; his seventeen children Rok, Miha, Liam, Marko, Benjamin, Simon, Dejan, Klemen, Luka, Jan, Mitja, Denis, Matej, Tej, Domen, Tomaž, and Bojan; his two nieces, Nika and Živa; and his pet tiger, Stripe.

IN MEMORY OF

Seth Dollars

January 13th, 1992 - May 7, 2013

HE TRIED TO INTERRUPT A POOPING BEAR

Seth Dollars of Paragould, Arkansas, was an avid camper. As part of our bear feces retrieval team, Dollars went out of his way to search forest floors for bear excrement to be brought back to our labs for processing. However, Dollars was so committed to his work that he continually sought to obtain fresher and fresher specimens. This came to a head when, one day in the Smoky Mountains of Tennessee, Dollars stalked a bear until it began its process of defecation, then attempted to run and slide beneath the bear with a catcher's mitt and capture a perfectly fresh mound of warm droppings. Unfortunately, Seth slid too far, nudged the bear in its unmentionables, and was mauled instantly.

Seth is survived by his father, Jesse; his mother, Penny; and his brother, Justin.

IN MEMORY OF

Melissa Bledsoe

December 25th, 1983 - July 1, 2018

TRIED TO BLIND TASTE TEST BEARS

Market researcher Melissa Bledsoe attempted to conduct blind taste tests with bears, trying to measure how accurately they could tell the difference between fresh, wild-caught salmon and the current vegan alternative. Bledsoe set up a table of samples in the Alaskan wilderness and awaited her test subjects. The moment one of the bears was given vegan salmon, the bear turned on Bledsoe; she lived up to her last name. Melissa's research was never recovered, but most agree that her tests proved unequivocally that bears are enraged by vegan salmon.

Bledsoe is survived by her husband, Pat Cummins, and her pets, Sir Elliott and Lady Violet.

IN MEMORY OF

Michael Avery Hardin

July 18th, 1978 - April 30, 2016

SHOULDN'T HAVE SPARRED WITH A BEAR

Boxing enthusiast Michael Avery Hardin from Bandon, Oregon, gave his heart, soul, and ultimately his life to researching the portion on bear fighting in this book. After months of training and preparation, Hardin invited a bear into his boxing gym by creating a trail of honey and salmon from the woods to his gym door. Once the bear was inside, Hardin invited it to join him in a sparring session, and the bear obliged. Michael unleashed his pugilistic expertise on the bear, but to no avail. The animal soon got a little too rough with Michael and knocked his head into the ocean. Michael's shih tzu, Moses, swam out to retrieve the head, which is now buried in Bandon Cemetery. Michael is survived by his dog, Moses; his cat, Little Debbie; his son, Nathan; and his wife, Megan.

IN MEMORY OF

Sam Holloway

December 19th, 1979 - September 13th, 2017

EXITED PURSUED BY A BEAR

Shakespearean actor Sam Holloway bravely attempted to test whether or not bears appreciated Shakespeare. Knowing bears would not accept humans as performers, Holloway went into the woods dressed in a lifelike bear costume to perform for the wild beasts. He performed for them Shakespeare's *Winter's Tale*. After his mask slipped, he attempted to exit the forest, but was pursued by bears and ultimately was slain. He was never able to document whether or not the bears had enjoyed the play up to that point; however, observers did attest to the bears' enjoyment of the unintended finale.

Sam is survived by his wife, Shana Matthews-Holloway, and son, Arthur Highlander Holloway (yes, that is his real middle name).

IN MEMORY OF

Paul Moore

August 26, 1977 - May 3, 2014

ATTEMPTED TO USE A BEAR AS A BASS AMP

Audio researcher Paul Moore went into the Russian mountains intending to prove his hypothesis that if he could plug his bass guitar into a sleeping bear, he could get the biggest, fattest, best tone any bassist has ever achieved. Moore succeeded in finding a bear in a deep sleep, and inserted a quarter-inch instrument cable jack into the bear's belly. He then plugged in his five-string Ibanez and started slappin' and poppin'. The resulting bass line sounded like the *Seinfeld* theme if it had been played by Zeus. Unfortunately, the mad funk woke the bear up and Paul Moore never returned from his journey.

Paul is survived by his daughter, Madison Moore, his five-string Ibanez, and his Mesa/Boogie full stack.

IN MEMORY OF

Scott Eno

January 1, 1968 - September 17, 2018

HE TRIED—AND FAILED—TO GET A BEAR SELFIE

Scott Eno was a dog lover, a hiker, and a talented photographer. Eno loved to hike in the woods and capture bears in their natural habitat with a high-powered lens. Eno took many of the photographs in this book, but over time he grew careless with the decreasing amount of space he put between himself and his subjects.

One day, while photographing bears just outside of his Virginia home, Scott decided to try to put himself in one of his own photos for once. This was his fatal mistake. Eno stood with his camera pointed at himself, with a bear in the distance about 500 feet away. Before the shutter even clicked, the bear was on him. The resulting photograph is one of the most disturbing selfies anyone has ever seen. It was so bad that Facebook's facial recognition attempted to match the image with uncooked meatloaf. Scott is survived by his wife, Sharon, and his dogs, Pecos, Yuki, and Dandy.

IN MEMORY OF

Bryan Lee Briggs

August 10th, 1974 - June 3, 2010

LIVE-ACTION ROLEPLAYING SHOULD NEVER INVOLVE BEARS

Bryan Lee Briggs worked in the IT department at the secret publishing facility where this book was tirelessly researched and written by thousands of dedicated bear researchers. However, in his spare time, Bryan Lee enjoyed live-action roleplaying.

Unfortunately, Bryan Lee allowed his live-action roleplaying adventures to take him to bear country where, despite his insistence that the bears were only roleplaying as harmless griffins, the bears attacked him anyway. The gun enthusiast fired thousands of rounds of ammunition at the bears, but was ultimately killed. Game over.

Bryan Lee Briggs is survived by his sister, Genevieve, and his guild, Willow, Travis, Tabitha, Liam, and Henry.

And to the many other slain bear research team members...

This book would not have been possible without the many researchers who went above and beyond the call of duty to record information that ultimately cost them all their lives.

Aaron "hugbear" Hughey
Aaron F Stanton
Aaron J
Aaron Smith
ABuczacki
Ace Cat.
Adam Bulleigh
Adam Huskins
Adam Rippon
ADAM STINES
Adrian Wells
Ajediday
akhliber
Ala
Alan Brookland
Alan Newman
Alex Tanner
Alex D
Alex Turnpenny
Alexander Nirenberg
Alexander Ornelas
Alison Liedkie
Amanda Hoapili
Andrea Martin
Andrew Bear
Andrew Cowie
Andrew Harootian
Andrew Irwin
Andrew Robertson
Andrew Shaw
Ant O'Reilly
Anthony C. Garcia
Anthony Townsend
Ashley Cox
Austin Haynes
B.A. Rosenblum
Barry Cope
Bart Stewart
Bear Food McCombs
Ben Brain
Ben Hanson
Ben Shepley
Benjamin Strauss
Beth McGrady
Bill Corbett
Blaž Brenčič
Bob & Jen Brinkman
Bob Loftus
Brad Sara
Bradley Weckman
Brandon Koepp
Brandon Sause
Brant Davidson
Brendan Bligh
Brett Perkins
Brian (Force) Weicker
Brian John
Brian Sandberg
Brian Saxon
Brian Shearer
Brien Dulaney
BRMK
Brock M

Bryan Johnson
Bryan Lee Briggs
Bryan Pusavat
Bryan Saulsbury
Bryant Shea
Caleb "Leyesyboy" Leyes
Cameron Belt
Cameron Emmons
Carl Allen
Carl Polzel
Carl Sondrol
Carla
Cdawg
Cecile Cloutier
Chad Dulin
Charles McDougald Jr.
Charlie Oliver
Charlie Tefft
Chloe Karr
Chris Beal
Chris Vangelder
Christen Bejar
Christian Hampson
Christian Kapsiak
Christina Gale
Christopher "I thought it was
a teddy" Brookes
Christopher "The Brave" Rider
Christopher Barron
Christopher Cowan
Christopher Davis
Clark Thomp
Clem Fandango
Cliff Cramp
Clyde Johns
Corey Booth
Craig 'KODIAKC' Black
CRob
Cryss BlackWolf
Crystal Bowman
D.R. McCale III
Damon & Peni Griffin
dan perry
Dan Roth
dangerdad
Daniel Morris
Daniel Pace
Daniel Parham
Darius Garsys
Dave Baxter
DaveSpeirs
David
David Altman
David Bass
David Chen
David Guzik
David Maxwell
David McGuire
David Nestingen-Palm
Dean McCaughan
Debbie Schwartz
Delaney Anderson
Derek Wells

Diablo Distro
Diana Weinstein Cauthen
Diandra Anne Lasrado
Gilberto Martinez
Dizzy D. Kelley
Don Tyler
Doug TenNapel
Douglas MacKrell
Douglas Young
Dr. Kevin Menard
Dr. Paul "Aaaah!" Auerbach
Dylan Marvin
e36freak
Ed Kowalczewski
Ed Lamb
Elena Neff (PuddleMilk)
Elias Baxter
EliOli Ceballos
Ellis Goodson
Eric Arsenault
Erik Ayres
Erik William Russell
Erikr
Erin&Jeremy Fuller
Ernie Griffin
Error_418_
Etakeh Oh
Ethan Baier
Ethan Dawson-Baglien
Etienne BEUREUX
F Jones
Field Marshall Liev, The
Viscount Skin
Filip -"lost my arm"- Liévois
Frank J. Fleming
Fred Hudson III
Gabriel Noronha Grecco
Garry Marlin
George
George Papantonopoulos
Gideon Dabi
Glen Sawyer
GM
Gordhan Rajani
Gordon Chen
Gordon Lindholm
greg carter
Greg Chag
greg kinney
Greg Tolle
Gregory Dalton
Gregory Paul Silber
Gretchen & Tucker
Gus Strand
Guy Bayes
hawkvictim
Heather Wilmes
Ilden
Iona "Literal Mothman" Spark
Ivan Otero
J Dunn
Jack Gulick
Jackie

Jacob darlington
Jairus Pascale
James & David C
James Jackman
James I. Delauder
James Lynch
James Morton
James Schledewitz
James Thomas
Jared G Miller
Jarrett Sacks
Jason Britton
Jason Chan
Jason Matty
Jeff & Sarah
Jeff Davis
Jeff Gray
jen philpot
Jennifer Moeller
Jeremey Lasher
Jeremiah Smith
Jeremy Kreutzer
Jeremy Lynch
Jeremy Rowland
Jeremy Turner
Jeremy Walling
Jett Bond
Jim Mortland
Jim Shepherd
Joanne Haagenson
Joel A Butler
Joey Hoit
Johannes Stauffer
John Aronis
John Carlos McMaster
John Famiglietti
John K Edwards II
John Merklinghaus
John Pasquini
john schnurr
John Wilson
Jon "Jolly" Rodgers
Jon Fenton
Jon Morin
Jon R. Alexander
Jonathan Grable
Jonathan Marshall
Jonathan Moore
Joseph Callister
Joseph J. Borrero
joseph mcconnell
Joseph Willaims
Joshua Carmody
Joshua McGinnis
Joshua Rice
Joshua Smutka
Justin Chamberlin
Justin James
Justin S. Davis
Kate "Grizzly" Adams
kathleen mitchell
Keith Clinkscales
Kel Poring

Ken Miller
Kenny Clem
Kevin Butler
Kevin Murphy
Kevin Schneider
Kevin Yong
KG Lacey
Khane A. Turner
Kim Scarborough
Kirk Spencer
KitsapGirl AKA Paula Sunkel
kokido
Kris Burr
Kristen MacLean
Kyle Cottengim
Kyle Mann
Kyle McCowin
Kyle Riley
Lady Tori "A Cool Ninja" Scott
Larry S.
Lars Brown
Laura Jeanne Bill
Lawrence Person
Lee P. Foley
Leif
Leszek NapieraÅ‚a
Lord Deathingtion
Lucas Gallagher
Lucha Jon
Luke D
Luke Peters
Lynn Wang
M. K. Kawai
Magan
Maj. James Weber, USAF
Manda Peacock
Manuel Neikov
Marc Whinston
Maria E Bartz
Marius Bjornstad
Mark Gustafson
Mark Jenkins
Mark Sorensen
Mark Swickard
Martin MacKinnon
Marty Akins
Mathew H. Farabee
Matt "snack cakes" Menefee
Matt Odell
Matt Shichtman
Matt Slatinsky
Matthew "Bear-Flattener" Sargent
Matthew Cinkoske
Matthew Edson
Matthew Loren Mo
Matthew Whittaker
McDonoughs
Medora Bennett
Melissa Bledsoe
Melissa Durrett
Michael
Michael "Necro Monkey" Schultz

Michael "Woodsman" Rief
Michael Faison
Michael Galica
Michael Grey
Michael Karcher
Michael Leal
Michael Orrin
Michael Shotwell
"Mighty" Walter McEuen
Miguel Angel Martinez
Miguel D. Serrano
Mike Hanson
Mike Palombi
Mike Parrish
Mike TechnoBear Weber
Milan Kovacs
Mirandia Berthold
Mitch Harding
Mitchel Ohman
MMC
Mohoganogan
Monte Carpenter
Mr Pudifoot
MurrayXmas
Nan "King of the Underworld"
Or
Nathan Blackham
Nathan Colacino
Nathaniel Cartoons
Neal Powell
Nicholas McCaskie
Nicholas Preece
Nick "Bear Spray" Dranias
Nick Fallon
Nick Lovell
Nick Vargish
Noah Nicole
Ordeithis
Paireon, lumberjack of Brimstone
paNik productions
Parry Pillsbury Gripp
Pat Gunn
Patricia Davidson
Patrick Finnen
Patrick McCarron
Patrick Petrashuyk-Weeks
Patrick Sennett
Patrick Walker
Paul Baumann
Paul Burch
paul d jarman
Paul Hackelberg
Paul Leone
Paul Moore
Pavel Morozov
Peat Ski
Perrydotto
Peter J. McHugh
Peter W. Horton Jr.
Philip Branting
Princess Selfrespectra
pw3ner
R.J Cochrane

Rachel "Dark One" Wise
Raemi Vrabel
Randall Cummings
Red Beard and Strawberry
Richard B. Smith, Jr.
Richard Ellis
Rick Henderson
Rick Tessner
Rico Alvarado
Rob
Robert Bowers
Robert Fouts
Robert Gilgan
Robert R. Herie Esq.
Roger Gebow
Roger John Davis
Russ The Love Bus
Ryan
Ryan C. Lowry
Ryan Emery
Ryan Lynch
Ryan Mikah Kutch
ryan north
Ryan Peterson
Ryan Riese
S. Koppelmann
Sakura Thompson
Sally Vorhies
Sam Holloway
Sam Maurer
Samuel Winfield
Sandy Germain Kottke
Sara Aitken
Sara Bryson
Scott Ryan-Hart
Scott Sibert
Scott Steubing
Sean Bodnar
Sean D
Sean M. Sickler
Sean McCormick
Sean Medlock
Sean Patrick Foley
Sean Whitley
Seth Dollars
Seth J. Morris
Seth Wood
Sexyblue
Shane Young
Shannon
Shannon Waldroop
Shawn Sneef
sillygoatgirl
Simon Shaw
Sogz
Sophie "Cherry Bomb" Hutchins
soxson
SP
Stan Brooks
Stephanie Carey
Stephen Spreng
Steve D
Steve Guiles

Steve Peters
Steven Alan Ford
Steven Callen
Steven Carpenter
Steven Shatz
Steven Shumaker
Stuart Owen
Sutter Cane
TBA Games
Ted Bear Graham
Theo Sanitate
Thermo
Thomas Fellrath
Thomas Nagle
Thomas Nicholson
Thomas Ryan
Thomas Saboy
Thomas W. Cox
Tiernan Douieb
Tierra Hedington
Tim Ellis
Tim Green
Tim La Rosa
Tim Sikes
Timothy VanKleeck
Timothy W. Youker
Tina Crowe
Todd A
Todd Levinson
Tom Badrick
Tomas Wynne
Tony Calidonna
Tracie Henderson
Tracy
Travis Dillon
Travis Kincher
Trevor Cooley
trevor huish
Tricia
Troy Martell
Vernon Ray Jackson
Vincci "$wag Money" Chung
Vince
Vince Pecoraro
Virginia Brown
Walter W.
Wan
Wanda Sherratt
Wardog Montana
Will Crawford
Will Gaffey
William
William and Barbara Ashton
William K
William V Turlik
Zac Edwards
Zoe Schuler

Thank You "Beary Much" For Your Service!

SPECIAL THANKS TO MY FRIENDS ON
PATREON

Patreon.com/EthanNicolle

a.r.
Aaron Guzman
Aaron Hughey
Acob Acob
Adam
Adam Brubaker
Adam Rippon
Adam Silverstein
Alberto
Alex Tanner
Alex Tongue
Alexei Kirtchik
Allison Hill
Amos Onn
Andrew LaSart
Andrey Sulemin
Angelito Villamena Jr
Angus Owen
Anthony Munoz
Argaen
ArtXpressME
Ashley Cox
Austin Short
Balinder Barard
Beastbot
BeeTee
Ben Norland
Benjamin
Benjamin Geile
Benjamin Gray
BERA Charles-Marie
Berry Newkirk
Bill Corbett
Bill Thomas
Bill Ã–berg
Blaž Brenčič

Brad Collins
Brandon Fox
Brandon Sause
Brendan Burch
Brian Loudon
Brian Tumbleston
Bryan
Caitlin Hyde
Caleb Leyes
Cameron Belt
Carl Polzel
Casey Carnahan
Cedric Hohnstadt
Charlie Haskins
Charlie J. Wall
Chelsea Roberts
Chris
Chris & Esther Cowan
Chris Hull
chris magee
Chris Wynter
Ciaran Mcloone
CiarÃin Kinsella
Cord Slatton-Valle
Corrigan
Cory Kerr
Craig Black
Curtis Charles
Dan Perry
Dan White
Daniel Fowler
Daniel Smartt
Dario Di Donato
Darius
Darrow Cole
David Altman

David Cooke
David Stafford
Dawn Wolf
Dean Stahl
Denis Nepveu
Diane Beggs
DISTRAKT
Don Tyler
Douglas Kim
Duncan Thomson
Duran Rivera
Dustin Montez
Dylan walsh
Ed Siomacco
Ederson Pereira
Eggsburst
Elliott Sims
Emily Adamson
Eric Porter
Eric Roesch
Eugene
FranÃ§ois-Denis
G. Strout
Gabelous
Gabriel
Gabriel Lee
Gannon Beck
Gareth Rogers
Geart
George Joseph Igel VI
George Papantonopoulos
George Spark-Stahl
Glen Piper
Glen Sawyer
Graham Finch

Greetings from Earth
Gregory Burrus
Gregory Dalton
Gregory Kinney
Gregory Silber
heyPert
Ilden Webber
Isaac
Isaiah Nicolle
Jacob Nelson
Jaime
James
James Kennison
Janis Allen
Janosch Jagi
Janusz Strzepek
Jared Westfall
Jason
Jason Brubaker
Jason Shaben
Jeff bauman
Jeff DeFouw
Jeff Walden
Jen Darmstadt-Holm
Jenn Chadek
Jeremy
jeremy kreutzer
Jess Pickert
Jimmy Parr
Jody Ingram
Joel Mills
Joel Wear
Joey Hoit
Joey Parrish
John Brunkhart
John Famiglietti
John Kessler

John Lockmer
John Merklinghaus
John Tinaglia
John Whelan
John-Andrew
O'Rourke
Jonathan Fenton
Jonathan Pratt
Jordan Kotzebue
Jorge A. Guandique
Jose
Jose Garibaldi
Joseph Hobbs
Josh Bluestein
Josh Gunderson
Josh Jackson
Joshua
Joshua Tukes
Josie Lynn
jrdsctt
Julien Lehoux
Justin Baglio
Justin S Davis
Kara Mia
Kazameltis
Keith
Kevin LaCoste
Kevin Vognar
Kristen Ford
Lachi
Linda Wilkins
lograh
Louis Badalament
Louis Mastorakos
Lr Cabarra
Lucas
Lucas Elliott
Luke Barnett
Luke Eperthener
Lurm

Marc Fletcher
Mark
Mark Chon
Mark Swanson
Martin Akins
Matt Menefee
matt sprankle
Matthew
Matthew Edson
Matthew K Hoddy
Matthuew Luse
Melissa Bledsoe
Michael D. Johas
Teener
Michael Regina
Michael Schultz
MichaÅ, KamiÅ,,ski
Mike Hanson
Milan Kovacs
Minzoku Bokumetsu
Mitch Harding
Moritz Herold
Myke Deneiko
Nathan Aardvark
Nathan Seabolt
Neal
Nicholas Hale
Wanchic
Nick Dranias
Niklas Emil Thorsen
Noeladoe
Obo
Omer Terry
OverviewBible
Panneer selvam
parthiban
Parry Gripp
Patrick Luther
Paul
Paul Ackerman

Paul Dufner
Paulie Godbout
Paulo Williams
Peter
Peter Gowen
Petit Professor
Pharoah Bolding
Phillip Liebold
Pop Mockers
Purpleflame
Rachel
Rachel Wintjen
Ralf Elizalde
Ralph Versteegen
Reagan Lodge
Rebekah Rivera
Richard
Rob Abrazado
Robert Groh
Robert Johnson
Ron Silva
Russell Frechette
Ryan Bettencourtt
Ryan Kutch
Ryan Peterson
Ryan Waldoch
Sal
Sally Vorhies
Sam Kressin
Sam Watkins
santosho
Sara Lopez
Shan
Wickremesinghe
Shane Ivey
Shane OReilly
Shark Gillins
Shea Kilgannon
Smith
smoochbelly

Stephen Young
Mr. Gee
Steven Shatz
Stew
Stew Taylor
Taggy
Tang
The Panduhs
The Power Boys
The Weapon
Creator
Theron Kantelis
Thomas Boguszewski
Thomas Cox
Thomas Oetker
Tim Ellis
Todd A
Tom
Tom Rogers
Trevor H. Cooley
Trevor Holoch
Van Evan Fuller
Vernon Jackson
Wade Goyens
Wanda Aasen
Wanda Sherratt
Wendy Caston
Wesley Scoggins
Whale Cry Games
Will Harwood
William Levinson
You Died Gaming!
Ziad WAKIM

If you enjoy my work, please consider giving my Patreon page a try. Patreon supporters get to see everything I make, long before it sees print. They get behind-the-scenes stuff, tutorials, commentaries, discounts, and all sorts of other bonus material from my many secret projects. You can join for as a little as $2/month.

-Ethan

ABOUT THE AUTHOR

Ethan Nicolle's first comic book series *Chumble Spuzz* (SLG Publishing 2007) was nominated for an Eisner Award for humor. He later created a web comic called *Axe Cop* with his little brother that became a viral sensation, which went on to become a Dark Horse comic book series and an animated series on FOX and FXX. Nicolle worked on the *Axe Cop* series as a writer, producer, voice actor, and creator. He has had multiple pitches optioned at Cartoon Network, and also worked as a staff writer and story editor on *VeggieTales in the House* at Dreamworks Animation, which was nominated for a Daytime Emmy. Nicolle has written for multiple animated TV series, including *Teen Titans Go!, Bunnicula,* and *Yabba Dabba Dinosaurs!* Ethan is also one of the writers and general photo-shoppers at the Babylon Bee, and publishes the ongoing web comic *Bearmageddon*. His first middle grade novel, *Ollie Possum,* will be released in 2019 from Canon Press. Ethan Nicolle is also known for illustrating Nick Offerman's books *Gumption* and *Good Clean Fun*.

OTHER CONTRIBUTORS

Cover, layout, graphics, etc.: Ethan Nicolle
Lead Editor: Sean Medlock
Additional Funny Stuff: Frank Fleming, Kyle Mann
Additional Proofing: Cryss Blackwolf, Debbie Schwartz, Brad Weckman, Danielle Smith, Beastbot, Kyle Riley, Bill Erickson, Gregory Silber

Written in large part while smoking fine cigars on the patio at **Pacific Wine Merchants in Upland, CA.**

Big thanks to those who spread the word, including...

Nick Offerman	Broman
Deborah Ann Woll	Robert Maguire
Stephanie Beatriz	Suzy Nakamura
Rifftrax	N'jaila Rhee
Jonah Goldberg	Gene Yang
Erix Metaxas	Rob Guillory
Todd Spence	Kevin Purdy
Doug TenNapel	Jon Gabriel
Jim Clemente	Sam Sykes
Harry Allen	Jim Treacher
Michelle Malkin	Tiernan Douieb
Alice R Fraser	MC Chris
Aaron Weiner	Steve Jackson Games
Jason Porath	Paul and Storm
Joe Randazzo	Erik Burnham
Tasha Robinson	Electric Gecko
Ryan Browne	Fox Force Five News
Chuck Wendig	Sanctum Secorum
Jamie Smart	Doug Culp
Mikey Neuman	Glen Fleishman
Marshall Julius	
Cade Peterson	

OTHER BOOKS BY
ETHAN NICOLLE

BEARMAGEDDON

This is the first volume collection of the web comic series Bearmageddon.

When Wow Mart employee Joel Morley and his slacker friends ditch society to live in the forest, they discover a mass exodus of bears heading into civilization to declare war on mankind. They enlist the help of a half-feral mountain man named Dickinson Killdeer to aid them in their quest to return to the city to find their families. However, with bears mutating, growing tentacles, and invading in massive numbers, it looks like the end of civilization as we know it.

"Bearmageddon wields a prescience that is both hilarious and terrifying, as Ethan Nicolle masterfully spells out the ursine demise that is coming to us all."
-**Nick Offerman** *(Parks & Rec, Axe Cop)*

DICKINSON KILLDEER'S GUIDE TO BEARS OF THE APOCALYPSE

A bear aficionado's field guide, written by the greatest bear fighter of all time, Dickinson Killdeer; includes illustrations by Ethan Nicolle and a foreword by Axe Cop himself. Profiles bear species from the bear elk to the mighty tribearatops.

AXE COP

(Six Volumes) The award-winning web comic created by Ethan Nicolle and his five-year-old brother about a cop with an axe. Volumes 1, 3, and 5 collect the webcomics, while 2, 4, and 6 collect print-exclusive storylines. Went on to become a FOX TV show starring Nick Offerman.

CHUMBLE SPUZZ

(Two Volumes) The Eisner-nominated series from SLG Publishing about two dimwits and their adventures involving devil pigs, Satan, feral humans, death, and cookies.

"For those of you who haven't read it, you should be making every possible effort to get your hands on it at all costs."
-**Jhonen Vasquez** *(Invader Zim)*

If you survived reading this book, please consider writing a review about it on Amazon!

Check out Ethan Nicolle's epic comic series Bearmageddon at:
www.Bearmageddon.com

Buy more bear stuff and find other works by Ethan Nicolle at:
www.AxeBearStore.com

THANK YOU